The Governor's Mansion of Texas

The
Governor's
Mansion
of
Texas

❖

*A Tour of Texas' Most
Historic Home*

Published and Edited
by
Friends of the Governor's Mansion
Austin

Friends of the Governor's Mansion is a Texas nonprofit corporation established November 1, 1979, for the benefit of the Governor's Mansion of Texas. The proceeds from the sale of this book provide funds for reprinting and for the continued maintenance of the contents and grounds of the Texas Governor's Mansion.

CREDITS FOR 1985 EDITION

Design/Production: Whitehead and Whitehead
Author: Dealey Decherd Herndon
Contributing Authors: Drury Blakeley Alexander,
   Audray Bateman Randle, Joe Frantz, and Jack Maguire
Photographers: Hickey Robertson Photography, Terry Duff, and
   Robert Anshutz
Architectural Drawings: Jim Hendricks
Printer: Communication Specialists, Inc.

CREDITS FOR 1997 EDITION

Editor for New Sections: Jane Karotkin
Production: Creatronics, Inc.
Photographer: Eric Beggs
Printer: The Whitley Company

FRIENDS OF THE GOVERNOR'S MANSION wishes to thank the following individuals for their special contributions to this book: Anne Alcorn, Joann Cook, Nancy Phyllis Crumpton, Anne DeBois, Debi Kendall, and Elizabeth Ann Morrow. FGM also wishes to thank Jan Bullock, Cissie Ferguson, Dealey Herndon, Karen Hughes, Margaret Marshall, Missy Rodgers, and Alice Sallee for their contributions to the second edition.

Contents

Introduction

WELCOME TO THE TEXAS GOVERNOR'S MANSION. Texas' most historic home has served as the official residence of the Texas governors and their families since 1856. It is the fourth oldest governor's mansion that has been continuously occupied in the United States, the older residences being those in Virginia, Mississippi, and Illinois. The Governor's Mansion belongs to all Texans and is opened to the public for tours.

The original construction of the Governor's Mansion was funded by state appropriations of $17,000. Work began in 1854 and was completed in the summer of 1856. Since that time, the state has retained responsibility for the house. Tight state budgets and changing economic conditions have combined to restrict funding. Both the exterior and interior have gone through long periods of deterioration followed by state commitments to implement necessary repairs and refurbishing. This limited funding has resulted in the remarkably preserved Greek Revival home that is seen today.

From 1965 to 1989, the Texas Commission on the Arts was responsible for the Texas Governor's Mansion and its contents through its Mansion Subcommittee. Since 1989, state law provides that the Texas Historical Commission is responsible for the preservation and maintenance of the Mansion and the protection of the historical and architectural integrity of the Mansion's exterior, interior, state-owned contents and grounds. The Texas Historical Commission has had the authority to review proposed architectural changes in the structure since the Mansion became a Texas Historical Landmark in 1962. In 1970, the United States Department of the Interior placed the Texas Governor's Mansion on the National Register of Historic Places and later designated it as a National Historic Landmark. The Texas General Services Commission maintains the structure and the grounds. The Mansion Administrator, representing the governor and first lady, oversees the day-to-day operations of the home.

FRIENDS OF THE GOVERNOR'S MANSION was established by Governor and Mrs. William P. Clements, Jr. in 1979 as a Texas nonprofit corporation for the benefit of the Texas Governor's Mansion. The proposed plan for the Mansion's first complete restoration and renovation had created a need for private funding and support. Although the state allocated $1,000,000 in 1979 to make necessary structural and maintenance changes in both the interior and exterior of the Governor's Mansion, there was no state funding for museum-quality furnishings and interior decoration. FRIENDS OF THE GOVERNOR'S MANSION, under the direction of a statewide board led by the late Mr. Ashley Priddy of Dallas, was successful in raising the money to achieve these goals.

On January 11, 1983, FRIENDS OF THE GOVERNOR'S MANSION established an endowment to assure ongoing maintenance of the Mansion Collection and to provide for educational projects such as this guidebook. FRIENDS OF THE GOVERNOR'S MANSION inventories and curates the furnishings and art in the public rooms of the Mansion, including state-owned pieces, under a contract with the Texas Historical Commission. This nonprofit organization is authorized to acquire additional items for use in the Mansion and provides seasonal plantings and special landscape improvements on the grounds.

The Texas Governor's Mansion has an exciting history. Each occupant has made a unique contribution to the story of this special home. Thanks to the people of Texas, the Texas Governor's Mansion today is a magnificent example of preservation at its best while remaining a home filled with the traditions and history of each governor's family.

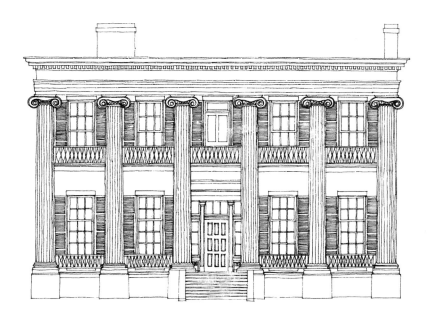

PART ONE

A Tour of the Mansion

The gracious, wide main hallway with its sixteen-foot ceilings and flowing stairway opens into each of the four original downstairs rooms of the Governor's Mansion, as well as into the 1914 addition at the far end. The window above the staircase originally opened to the outside.

On the north wall of the Entry Hall is a ommode in the French taste, suggesting the work of Emmons and Archibald of Boston, circa 1815–1820. Above the commode hangs an exquisite Louis Clapier pier mirror that was purchased ftom the Clapier descendants and was exhibited in the Philadelphia Museum of Art in 1976 as part of a six-month exhibition, Three Centuries of American Art.

Entry Hall

*F*ROM THE WIDE FRONT PORCH, visitors enter the Texas Governor's Mansion through the original doorway that Abner Cook built in 1856. The basic floor plan of the Mansion was designed to take advantage of Texas' summer breezes. In the 1856 house, all downstairs rooms opened to this center hall. On hot summer days, the exterior doors could be opened in front and back, allowing for pleasant ventilation.

The Entry Hall has changed very little since 1856. The wide-plank pine flooring was added in the 1979–1982 restoration-renovation to reproduce the original flooring. The keyhole molding around the windows and doors is original, as is the graceful arched stairway with its walnut balustrade. Early photographs of the Mansion show the area under the stairway both enclosed and open at various times during the Mansion's history. The far wall to the south of the stairway has been rounded off to conceal modern ductwork.

The focal point of the room is the sweeping stairway. Throughout the history of the house, children have enjoyed sliding down the long, circular railing of the staircase to the hall below. Governor Jim Hogg nailed tacks the length of the banister to prevent further mishaps following an accident to his youngest son during the Hogg administration (1891–1895). The filled nail holes are still visible in the railing today.

Furnishings have varied with the times and the tastes of the occupants. During the earliest years of its history, the Mansion was sparsely furnished. Texas was a young frontier state with scarce funding, and it was necessary to travel long distances for delivery of goods and furnishings. Locally available hide-covered chairs and cotton rugs were at home in the Mansion. Other furnishings have been described as "plain and neat." During most

One of a rare matched pair of American New York Regency consoles or pier tables. The tables of figured rosewood embellished with delicate inlays of brass and accented with carved giltwood ornaments are attributed to Duncan Phyfe, New York, circa 1825.

The Entry Hall doorway is framed with keyhole molding used by builder Abner Cook throughout the house. Above each Regency console is a fine American Federal girandole mirror, crested by a spread-winged eagle holding a ball and chain.

3

The American Empire sofa, attributed to New York cabinet-maker Duncan Phyfe, displays acanthus foliage in the design of its curved arms. The graceful arms flow into heavily carved legs and paw feet. On the Classical hexagonal card table beside the sofa is a cut crystal mantel lamp with a bronze base and etched shades.

of the twentieth century, the floors of the Mansion were covered with wall-to-wall carpeting, and the walls were papered. In the 1930s, the Entry Hall displayed many of the historic paintings that still hang in the Mansion.

In April 1982, when the Mansion officially reopened after the 1979–1982 restoration-renovation, the Entry Hall had been completely refurnished. The Senna Kurd rug, the stairway rug designed to complement it, and the twelve-arm crystal chandelier (1860) were acquired through FRIENDS OF THE GOVERNOR'S MANSION and donated to the State of Texas by a Texas foundation. The furnishings represent the work of Duncan Phyfe (the sofa, side tables, and consoles) and Louis Clapier (the mirror). Appropriate American pieces were acquired by FRIENDS OF THE GOVERNOR'S MANSION to complete the redecoration of the Entry Hall.

The most significant piece in the Governor's Mansion hangs in the Entry Hall. *Fall of the Alamo*, an historical painting by Robert Jenkins Onderdonk, is a nationally recognized work. Painted around 1903 after careful research by the artist, it is considered the most authentic artistic depiction of the event in existence and has been included in many Texas history textbooks. The painting was donated to FRIENDS OF THE GOVERNOR'S MANSION by two Houston families in 1981. *Fall of the Alamo* hangs in this prominent place in the Mansion as a reminder of the unique history of Texas.

Fall of the Alamo, *by Robert Jenkins Onderdonk, is considered to be one of the most authentic paintings of the famous battle at the Alamo in 1836. Onderdonk, who lived and worked the greater part of his adult life in San Antonio, researched the clothing, weapons, and the battle itself to make his historical work as authentic as possible.*

Small Parlor

Oil portrait of Sam Houston as a young man, painted by artist Martin Johnson-Heade (1819–1904).

T HE SMALL PARLOR to the north of the front door has been used for formal entertaining since the Mansion was completed in 1856. Governors and first ladies have received their guests in this room over the years. Marcelle Lively-Hamer, the author of a brochure on the Mansion during the Allred administration, referred to this room as the "Reception Suite." The room has retained its original dimensions and exposures. The only significant changes were decorative additions to the room. In the early twentieth century, the parlors were made more formal by adding plaster cove moldings at the ceiling, changing the mantel to an elegantly carved design, and including a large tilted overmantel mirror. This mantel probably replaced a simpler mantel like the one now in the Mansion Library.

Through the years, this room has been sparely and inconsistently furnished. Governor and Mrs. Pease were allocated only $2,500 to furnish the entire house when it was completed in 1856. The Peases used their own furnishings in the house, and

5

The elegant mirrored overmantel in the Small Parlor reflects the beauty of this formal entertaining area. Flanking the fireplace is a pair of handsome mahogany upholstered klismos armchairs, Philadelphia, circa 1830–1835.

this practice was continued through the years as a means of filling the Mansion rooms and providing for comfortable living.

As a small frontier town, Austin was not suited to formal entertaining when the Mansion first opened. Guns and muddy boots were common parts of the male attire so the parlors were probably filled with practical furnishings suited to the customary visitor.

As Texas became more prosperous and railroad transportation to Eastern markets became available, finer furnishings became accessible and were doubtless used in the parlors of the Governor's Mansion. Mrs. Orline (Lena) Sayers, first lady at the turn of the century, added formal architectural details to the parlors and purchased more formal furnishings, including gilt French chairs and reproduction French cabinets, which remained in the Mansion through most of the twentieth century.

In 1975, Miss Ima Hogg, who had lived in the house as a child and who later became the Mansion's earliest benefactor, loaned the Mansion a ten-piece set of Belter furniture and arranged for

Sam Houston's portrait hangs in a prominent place in the Mansion's Small Parlor. A stately Empire sofa faces the fireplace.

In the Small Parlor, an American Regency or Federal period "bulls-eye" mirror hangs above a Sheraton bowfront commode, attributed to William Hook, circa 1800–1815. An unusual pair of black and white French Empire campana, or bell-shaped, vases is displayed on the commode. The portrait of Hermann Lungkwitz is by Friedrich Richard Petri. Lungkwitz and Petri were artists who immigrated to Texas from Germany in 1851.

This museum-quality mahogany Sheraton serving table, circa 1800–1810, is attributed to a famous Salem, Massachusetts, furnituremaker, William Hook. Above the Hook table hangs a bluebonnet oil painting by Texas artist Julian Onderdonk, the son of the artist who painted Fall of the Alamo in the Entry Hall.

7

An American piano-forte made by T. Nielson. The instrument is in an ornate mahogany case with gilt and brass mounts.

the loan of an additional twelve pieces of Belter-style, laminated rosewood furniture. The twenty-two pieces were to be used together, with the matched sets undivided, until a permanent collection of appropriate antiques could be acquired. This set, which included chairs, tables, and sofas, was used in the parlors until 1980 when they were returned to the Houston Museum of Fine Arts and the San Antonio Museum Association as specified in the loan agreements.

Today, the Small Parlor is furnished with one of the country's finest collections of nineteenth-century American antiques. Most of the pieces seen in the Small Parlor today were acquired by FRIENDS OF THE GOVERNOR'S MANSION during the 1979–1982 Mansion restoration-renovation. With few exceptions, most notably the Martin Johnson-Heade portrait of Sam Houston, the pieces were collected specifically for the room and were produced in America in the early 1800s by skilled craftsmen. The area rugs were specially designed for the room and made in America of natural fibers. The draperies are patterned after period Federal window treatments.

Large Parlor

*T*HE LARGE PARLOR has been the gathering place for many formal events, both official and personal. The room has been the setting for several weddings, with the wedding party gathering around the mantel. The room has remained basically unchanged through the years, with the exception of the addition of the plaster cove molding, the carved mantel, and the mirrored overmantel. First Lady Janey Briscoe added the large, English crystal chandeliers in 1978, replacing the smaller ones that now hang in the Upstairs Hall.

The two parlors often function as one large entertaining area. The rugs are different yet complementary. The draperies and English crystal chandeliers are identical in each room as is the architectural detailing.

French cabinetmaker and artisan Charles-Honoré Lannuier came to New York in the 1790s. This magnificent Empire card table, circa 1810, is attributed to Lannuier. The lyre base is capped with gilded swans' heads.

9

This view of the northwest corner of the Large Parlor shows the distinctive architectural detailing—the mantel with its overmirror, the cove molding at the ceiling, and the keyhole window molding. The portrait on the far wall is of Governor Richard Coke, painted ten years after his administration (1874–1876).

The carving on this Sheraton sofa is attributed to Samuel McIntyre, Salem, Massachusetts, circa 1810. The crest rail has carvings of wheat and flowing grapevines.

One of an exquisite Worcester garniture set consisting of three matching campana, or bell-shaped, vases with loop handles, circa 1820.

As in the Small Parlor, the majority of the furnishings in the Large Parlor were acquired by FRIENDS OF THE GOVERNOR'S MANSION as part of the restoration-renovation. Notable exceptions are the Governors' Collection and the portraits of Governor and Mrs. Richard Coke (1874–1876) which hung in this location in the 1930s. The finest available American-made antiques were sought for this room—and other rooms throughout the house— to supplement the Mansion Collection. In the Large Parlor, the Sheraton sofas, one attributed to Duncan Phyfe and the other to Massachusetts woodcarver Samuel McIntyre, create a central seating area completed by intricately carved Empire and Federal chairs and tables. A museum-quality carved and gilded card table by nineteenth-century cabinetmaker Charles Lannuier was purchased for the north wall. The fine, Hepplewhite tall clock represents the Willard school of clock making at its finest.

Of particular interest to Texans are the four William Henry Huddle landscapes of Austin in the 1880s. The set includes the oil paintings: *Barton Creek, Bull Creek, A View of Austin,* and an unidentified *Lagoon.* A noted Austin artist, Huddle also painted portraits of the nineteenth-century governors. These portraits hang in the Gallery of Governors in the Texas State Capitol.

The opening between the two parlors has been restored to reflect its early character. Through the years, several architectural designs and decorative trims had been applied to the opening. The draperies are period reproductions and have been hung inside the window mold so that the full effect of the original key-

A portion of the Governors' Collection is contained in this mahogany Empire breakfront, attributed to Joseph Barry of Philadelphia, circa 1815–1825.

This fine American, four-piece, silver tea service was made by Fletcher and Gardner of Philadelphia, circa 1812. It rests on a tray by Baldwin Gardiner, New York, circa 1830. The center is engraved with armorials of John Jay, signer of the Declaration of Independence for the State of New York.

hole detailing can be appreciated. The rugs were designed to coordinate the two parlors, replacing wall-to-wall carpeting that had been used in this area during recent history. Custom-cast, "Lone Star" drapery tie-backs were made for all the Mansion windows.

The parlors contain a unique collection of fine accessories. Most notable in this room is the rare American-made tea service which rests on a signed silver tray, displaying the armorials of John Jay, signer of the Declaration of Independence.

Library

THE LIBRARY remains basically unchanged since the Mansion was constructed. The mantel was copied for other rooms during the recent restoration-renovation since it was considered the only original mantel in the house and is similar in design to mantels seen in other Austin houses built by master builder Abner Cook. At various times, the room has been called the "Library," the "Reading Room," the "Southeast Drawing Room," and the "Green Room," the latter because it has been decorated in various shades of green.

When Governor Pease first moved into the newly constructed Mansion in June 1856, he wrote to his wife Lucadia in Connecticut.

I have arranged the southeast corner room, or reading room, as I suppose we shall call it, as follows. The large looking glass and pier table are between the two windows on

The Library is painted a warm green, based on research indicating a history of decorating the room in various shades of green. The Library mantel is original and was reproduced in other rooms during the 1979–1982 restoration-renovation. The portrait of Stephen F. Austin has hung in the Mansion for many years. The pair of Bergère gentlemen's armchairs was acquired during the Allred administration (1935–1939).

A Classical mahogany shelf clock with original èglomisé, the French term for a special type of reverse painting on glass that is backed with gold-leaf or silver-leaf foil. Inscribed, "Aaron Willard, BOSTON," circa 1815–1820.

the east or front side, the book case that stood in the hall is between the door and the front window, the new book case is between the chimney and the side next the hall in the recess, the table that stood in the parlor stands in the center of this room, the clock and ornaments are to stand on the mantle, and Jenny Lind is to front the fireplace just as she did in the parlor, how do you like my taste in arranging the room?

Since that time, this room has been used primarily as a library or study, but it has occasionally been a bedroom. In 1941 when Governor Coke Stevenson moved into the Mansion with his terminally ill wife, he converted the Library, or Green Room, into a bedroom and closed up the South Entry to add a small downstairs bathroom. First Lady Blanch Fay Stevenson died in the Green Room on January 3, 1942, just five months after her husband took office. The South Entry remained closed until the restoration-renovation, and the area provided the only powder room for guests from 1941 until 1982.

The contents of the Library reflect Texas history as well as Mansion history. A portrait of Stephen Fuller Austin hangs over the mantel. Known as the "Father of Texas," Austin brought the first American colonists to Texas. Three hundred families settled in an area of south Texas around the Colorado and Brazos river bottoms. The capital of the new colony was named San Felipe de Austin after its founder and leader. After serving as the first secretary of state of the Republic of Texas, Stephen F. Austin died in 1836. Twenty years later, the Governor's Mansion was completed, and his portrait hangs here as a tribute to his part in Texas history.

In 1923, the Stephen F. Austin desk was bequeathed to the Mansion by his sister's heirs. Austin had used the desk when visiting in his sister's home in Peach Point. On top of the desk is a candelabrum depicting Davey Crockett with the Indians.

Other historical pieces in the Library include the sofa which belonged to Governor E.M. Pease and his wife Lucadia, the first residents of the Mansion, and the pair of chairs by the fireplace, which were acquired for the Mansion by First Lady Joe Betsy Allred. The statue of William Jennings Bryan is the work of Austin sculptress, Elisabet Ney, during the Sayers administration (1899–1903). Bryan was a friend of Governor and Mrs. Sayers, as was Elisabet Ney, and visited the Mansion.

The Library bookcases are the only new pieces acquired during the Mansion restoration-renovation. After an extensive search for a pair of period bookcases proved fruitless, a smaller pair of bookcases in the library of the General Dodge home in Council Bluffs, Iowa, was reproduced for this location. The bookcases are a testament to the fact that excellence in cabinetmaking still

A magnificent pair of American-made reproduction bookcases and the Stephen F. Austin desk set the mood in the Governor's Mansion Library. On top of the bookcase is a bust of William Jennings Bryan by Austin sculptress Elisabet Ney. A signed and dated (1848) silver-plated candelabrum, "Davey Crockett and the Indians," is on the Austin desk.

The silver plaque on this walnut fall-front desk with burl panels reads: "Desk used by General Stephen F. Austin at Peach Point, the home of his sister, Mrs. Emily M. Perry, and presented to the State, June 7, 1923. Neff administration."

The Library's four-branch brass chandelier with etched glass hurricanes and long prisms has hung in its original location since the turn of the century.

Descendents of Governor and Mrs. E. M. Pease donated the Pease American Empire sofa to the State of Texas. Beside the sofa is a period sewing table with its upholstered lower basket for yarns, needles, thread, or fabric. A lyre base table with brass claw feet and casters serves as a tea table in front of the sofa.

exists in this country. Many of the books are on loan from the University of Texas Texana Collection, and a few belong to the Mansion Collection.

The historic green theme has been retained in the Library. The walls are now painted, replacing the wallpaper treatment that was prominent in the twentieth century. As in the other public rooms, the period draperies have been set inside the distinctive original keyhole molding. The doorway to the right of the fireplace has been closed to create storage for the State Dining Room.

State Dining Room

THE STATE DINING ROOM has been consistently used for official state dinners since the Governor's Mansion was built. In this room, governors have discussed the most critical state issues with officials and dignitaries as well as with their own families. The governors celebrated the holidays with their families in this room, and that tradition continues today.

Just as the other rooms reflected the pioneer character of Texas in the early days, so did the dining room. In 1856, the furnishings were scarce and simple. The house ended at the back wall of the room, and a large basement with steps from the backyard was located directly under this room. The 1914 addition created the openings from the dining room into the newly constructed Conservatory.

The walls have been painted as well as papered through the years. First Lady Mildred Moody (1927–1931) covered the walls with a Zuber wallpaper entitled "Scenic America." It depicted this nation in the late 1700s. This was replaced by a red-flocked wallcovering during the Shivers administration. The red theme remained until the Clements redecoration when the walls were again painted as in the early years. The window treatment has changed as tastes changed and money became available. Large mirrored overmantels hung over both fireplaces for much of the twentieth century. They were removed in 1980, and the mantels were restored as near as possible to their original character.

A formal Mansion place setting includes state china and silver, both of which bear the Texas State Seal.

The State Dining Room will accommodate eighteen guests at the oval mahogany Sheraton Regency dining table. The six-branch brass chandelier, patented April 1, 1843, by C. Cornelius and Sons of Philadelphia, was acquired during the Briscoe administration.

Portrait of John Wharton in military uniform. He and his brother, William, were contemporaries of Sam Houston and served in the Republic of Texas Diplomatic Corps.

One of the State Dining Room's two fireplaces is on the west wall, the back wall of the Mansion until the 1914 addition.

One of two armchairs that are part of a rare set of twelve Classical mahogany dining chairs with upholstered slip seats, New York, circa 1815.

This Sheraton mahogany serving table, circa 1800–1810, is attributed to cabinetmaker William Hook of Salem, Massachusetts. Above the server is the landscape Texas Military Institute, Austin *painted by Hermann Lungkwitz in 1874.*

Naturalistic flower painting on Derby urns with original gilding and fire cracks, circa 1810–1820.

Several pieces seen in the State Dining Room were purchased for the Mansion with the assistance of Miss Ima Hogg, the only daughter of Governor James Hogg. The mahogany banquet table was acquired in 1943. The American Sheraton sideboard was donated by her that year, and this sideboard is perhaps the oldest American-made piece in the house. Miss Hogg also gave a fine pair of porcelain vases in 1943 during the Stevenson administration.

The portraits in the State Dining Room are reminiscent of early Texas. The Wharton brothers, John and William, were diplomats during the days of the Texas Republic and were con-temporaries of Sam Houston. These paintings have been a part of the Mansion Collection for many years.

Governor and Mrs. Allan Shivers (1949–1957) established offi-cial state silver and china collections which are still used today. Each governor has had the opportunity to add to the state silver pattern, "Pointed Antique" by Reed and Barton. The state seal is engraved on the front of the silver, and the name of the governor in whose administration the piece was acquired is engraved on the back. The state china is the "Jefferson" pattern by Pickard China, decorated with the state seal in gold.

The State Dining Room is decorated in rich blues and reds to complement the Persian Tabriz rug, circa 1925–1930. A rare set of twelve Federal dining chairs and a similar set of six Empire chairs attributed to New York cabinetmaker Duncan Phyfe allow seating for up to eighteen guests at the table for Mansion enter-taining. The two fireplaces and their chimneys were restored during the 1979–1982 restoration-renovation.

The American Sheraton sideboard, circa 1790, on the north wall was a gift from Miss Ima Hogg. A large girandole, or convex mirror, with a magnificent carved and gilded frame hangs above the sideboard.

A heavily carved Duncan Phyfe table and a set of ten mahogany klismos chairs (New York, circa 1815) create an informal dining area. The seals of Spain, France, Mexico, Texas, the Confederacy, and the United States are incorporated into the Conservatory rug. More than thirty colors create the seals and Texas wildflower designs.

Classical box sofa with straight column front, decorative gilding, and brass caster feet, circa 1820.

Conservatory

THE CONSERVATORY was created as part of the 1914 addition to the Governor's Mansion. It has served as a less formal dining room for the governor's family and friends since it was first built. Through the years, it has been decorated more casually than the rest of the house and has often been called the "Family Dining Room."

As the state grew and the need for formal entertaining increased, the Conservatory became not only a family room but an entertaining room as well. During the 1979–1982 restoration-renovation, this dual use was the primary consideration when determining the contents of the room.

The wide expanse of windows is only partially curtained, admitting light and a view of the gardens. A shade of soft yellow complements the room's carved Empire furniture, and a colorful rug has a design of Texas wildflowers and the seals of the six nations that have ruled the state. The theme for the rug was suggested by Governor Bill Clements.

A large gilt mirror with the Texas State Seal hangs in the Conservatory and was a gift to the Mansion from Temple Houston

The large gilded mirror with the Texas State Seal hangs above the burl-walnut veneer Empire sideboard. The mirror was carved by Dallas woodcarver August F. Strohmeyer around 1900. The State Official Ladies Club donated the handsome antique silver coffee urn to the Mansion in 1958.

This fine American breakfront secretaire *was purchased by* FRIENDS OF THE GOVERNOR'S MANSION *to house a portion of the Governors' Collection.*

A comfortable seating area in the Conservatory allows versatile use of the room for gatherings and meetings as well as for dining.

Morrow, a grandson of Sam Houston. A portion of the Governors' Collection is housed in a magnificent *secretaire* on the east wall. The American *secretaire* has intricately carved mullions on the glass doors, a veneered fan motif repeated on the fall front and the cabinet section below, and bow-fronted cabinets and drawers.

Several pieces of the Mansion silver collection are displayed in this room. Governor and Mrs. Allan Shivers began the tradition of giving and accepting silver pieces to form a fine collection for the Mansion. This tradition has been continued during subsequent administrations.

Back Entry

THE BACK ENTRY has evolved over the years to the gracious wide hallway that is seen today. This area at one time was a covered outdoor porch which provided shelter for the servants coming to and from the semidetached kitchen to the north. The entire back of the original Mansion consisted of an L-shaped porch which ran along the back of the dining room and turned to join the kitchen wing. In this stately brick home, the original floors in the main house were of seasoned pine, but the separate

26

This view of the Back Entry shows the doorway with its glass panels and transom. Plant stands carved with the Texas State Seal flank the door. The red, white, and blue area rug closest to the door shows the seldom seen reverse side of the Texas State Seal design with the star, the six flags, and the Alamo. The Malmaison bookcase on the left contains the Mansion's **Texian Campaigneware** *Collection.*

The Mocking Bird *was drawn from nature by John James Audubon. The mockingbird is the Texas state bird. This chromolithograph of Audubon's drawing was done by B.J. Bien in 1860.*

kitchen had a dirt floor. Adjoining the porch was a cistern that provided fresh rainwater for the Mansion residents.

In 1914, the only major addition to the Mansion created this area. At that time, a hallway was constructed between the new Conservatory and the new kitchen, butler's pantry, and service areas. The 1914 addition was fully attached to the original house but was more functional than gracious. The front door remained the official entrance to the house. Over the years, the Back Entry with its wide, accessible driveway became more and more commonly used to enter the Mansion. Still, the back hallway was too narrow to be decorated for use as part of the formal entertaining area in the Mansion.

The 1979–1982 restoration-renovation included changes to provide a more suitable reception area at the back of the house. The area was widened to the dimensions seen today, and the ceilings were raised to a height complementary to the other rooms. The openings into the area were adjusted to suit a gracious entryway.

27

The initials "J. B.," which appear on the Mansion Collection Texian *plates under the familiar cartouche, indicate that they were made by potter James Beech. He began producing the* Texian Campaignware *for the American markets between 1846 and 1848. Two other potters, Thomas Walker and Anthony Shaw, entered the market later.*

The Governor's Mansion has acquired an outstanding collection of commemorative earthenware that is displayed in the Back Entry. *Texian Campaigneware* was made in northern Staffordshire, England, from 1846 until approximately 1852, to commemorate the war between the United States and Mexico (1846–1848). It was underglazed in traditional Staffordshire blue as well as in several other colors. The uniforms and settings depicted are unrealistic; the romanticized battle-scene designs were probably taken from European battle drawings rather than adapted from American lithographs.

The Back Entry has two area rugs, one with the reverse side of the Texas State Seal and the other showing the state bird, the mockingbird. An Audubon print of the mockingbird hangs above the mahogany Sheraton serving table attributed to Duncan Phyfe, circa 1815. With such other additions as prints of the Mexican War (1846–1848), hand carvings of the state seal on matching mahogany pedestals, and a unique collection of *Texian Campaigneware*, the Mansion now has an attractive Back Entry that reflects the history of Texas.

28

Upstairs Hail

T HE UPSTAIRS HALL displays a significant part of the state-
owned Mansion Collection. Throughout the twentieth century, these pieces were given by generous Texans to the Mansion
and the State of Texas. The chandeliers were probably acquired
by First Lady Lena Sayers (1899–1903) for the downstairs parlors.
They hung there for more than seventy years until First Lady
Janey Briscoe moved them upstairs and replaced them with a
larger pair. The Rumanian rug of oriental design was a gift to the
Mansion in 1978 during the Briscoe administration.

From the early days of the Governor's Mansion, the Upstairs
Hall served two functional purposes. Since the window above the
stairway originally opened to the outside and the east door
opened to the balcony, the hallway served as a cooling breezeway
in the hot Texas summers. The hallway also provided a central

*The Mallard sofa,
Belter armchairs, and
Mallard side chairs
form a comfortable
seating area in the
hallway The tiered,
crystal-prism chande-
lier is one of a pair
that hung for seventy
years in the down-
stairs parlors. The
Private Quarters are
behind the original
1856 window in
the stairway.*

29

This view of the Upstairs Hall shows two Belter side chairs and a Belter table in front of the heavily draped balcony door. The elaborate Brussels longcase clock was given to the Mansion in 1943. The gold leaf pier mirror with console was donated to the Mansion in 1973 by relatives of Governor and Mrs. Charles Culberson (1895–1899).

This Victorian armchair, with intricately carved and laminated rosewood from the Rococo Revival period, is one of a six-piece set (circa 1850) attributed to John H. Belter. The set was bequeathed to the Governor's Mansion by Miss Ima Hogg during the Briscoe administration.

30

gathering area or sitting room between the four original bedrooms.

After the cross ventilation was blocked by the 1914 addition, Governor James Ferguson (1915–1917) screened the balcony as a sleeping porch, and the hallway provided the only access to this area. The balcony remained screened for at least four decades.

Most governors' families have used the Upstairs Hall as a sitting room. The major exception was the period from the Shivers administration until the Briscoe administration when the hallway was divided from north to south to provide an office for the First Family. The dividing partition was on the east side of the door into the only official state bedroom, called the "Sam Houston Bedroom," at that time. This allowed visitors to tour the state bedroom without entering the Private Quarters and left the official state bedroom as part of the public Mansion. Governor and Mrs. Briscoe restored the hallway to its original character.

Victorian Belter and Mallard pieces seen in the Upstairs Hallway were given to the Mansion by Miss Ima Hogg. The sofa and matching chairs are attributed to nineteenth-century New Orleans craftsman Prudent Mallard. Four chairs and the intricately carved Victorian table are credited to New York cabinetmaker John Henry Belter (1804–1863). A large oil painting, *Richard Barwell and Son,* painted by Sir Joshua Reynolds, was a gift to the Mansion during the Shivers administration and now hangs above the Mallard sofa. The elaborate longcase clock was a favorite of First Lady Ima Mae Smith who had it restored and put in working order. Legend suggests that it once belonged to Napoleon I of France. The chest on the north wall belonged to Governor John Ireland and First Lady Anne Maria Ireland when they were in the Mansion (1883–1887) and was a gift to the state in 1969. An ornate gold-leaf rococo mirror, a gift to the state during the Jester administration (1947–1949), hangs above the Ireland chest.

This burl-walnut chest with marble top was owned by Governor and Mrs. John Ireland (1883–1887). It was used in the Mansion and was a gift to the state in 1969.

Pease Bedroom

THIS BEDROOM was officially named the Pease Bedroom in 1982 during the Clements administration to honor the first occupants of the Governor's Mansion, Governor Elisha Marshall Pease and First Lady Lucadia Pease (1853–1857, 1867–1869). In this bedroom are several pieces that belonged to the Peases, including the two beds, the desk used by the Peases in the Mansion, and the portraits. The clock belonged to the descendants of Governor and Mrs. Pease. A copy of the invitation to the first

Governor Elisha Marshall Pease looks out at the room named in his honor from the portrait above the restored fireplace and mantel. The Pease portraits were donated to FRIENDS OF THE GOVERNOR'S MANSION *by his descendants and were meticulously restored by the Kimbell Museum.*

These magnificent four-poster beds belonged to Governor and Mrs. Pease and are thought to have been used in the Governor's Mansion during their stay (1856–1857). The coverlets were hand-quilted with tone-on-tone designs reminiscent of the State of Texas.

official Mansion party, or *levee,* is in this room. Governor Pease invited all of Austin to the Mansion in August of 1856 while Mrs. Pease was visiting relatives in the east with their daughters.

This southwest bedroom was designated as the first official state bedroom by First Lady Lena Sayers (1899–1903), and the Sam Houston bed became the central feature. This room served as a bedroom for state guests and was often opened to public tours. It remained the "Sam Houston Room," with repeated redecoration to reflect current styles, until 1982.

The Pease Bedroom floors, as all of those in the public Mansion, were restored to the original wide-plank pine during the

Empire teapot presented to Lieutenant Colonel Charles Ruff upon his retirement from the army in 1864. The engraving lists the seven major battles of the Mexican-American War in which Ruff fought and played a major role.

This Texas-made walnut American Empire wardrobe has three drawers in the center and a dome panel door on either side of a hand-beveled mirror.

A family portrait of First Lady Lucadia Pease hangs in the Pease Bedroom above the Victorian sofa.

restoration-renovation. The rug was handwoven in New England to repeat the design in the drapery fabric. The muslin quilts were handstitched to illustrate Texas themes: the Mansion, Sam Houston on his horse, bluebonnets, the Indian paintbrush wildflower, and the Texas State Seal.

The wardrobe is considered the finest Texas-made piece in the Mansion and was featured in Lonn Taylor and David Warren's *Texas Furniture.* It is often referred to as the "Sayers Armoire" since it was restored and returned to the Mansion by First Lady Lena Sayers at the turn of the century. It has remained in the Mansion since that time and was possibly used in the house years earlier. The wardrobe is one of the few pieces in the Mansion that has been retained through the years, giving it a special historic significance. The Belter sofa and the pair of Mallard armchairs are part of the two sets in the hallway, gifts of Miss Ima Hogg.

The bathroom and dressing area are part of the 1914 addition. Until that time, there was no bathroom serving the Pease bedroom. Running water had been added to the Governor's Mansion in 1883, primarily as a fire prevention measure. The 1853 Capitol had burned on November 9, 1881, creating concern about other state buildings. Bathroom facilities have been gradually upgraded through the years.

The pieces shown in this photograph of the Pease Bedroom have belonged to the State of Texas for many years. The slant-top walnut Pease family desk on the far wall was retrieved from the Capitol basement, restored, and returned to the Mansion to become an integral part of the Pease Bedroom. On top of the desk is an invitation to the Mansion's first party on August 23, 1856. On the reverse side of the invitation is a copy of a handwritten letter from Governor Pease to his wife, describing the event. The mahogany Biedermeier-style chest in the foreground was originally purchased in New Orleans in 1850 and was given to the Mansion in the 1970s. Above it hangs a late Empire mirror that can be seen in Mansion photographs as early as 1925.

Sam Houston Bedroom

*Sam Houston pur-
chased this handsome
four-poster canopy bed
for the Governor's
Mansion. "Superior
Bed Stead, mahogany"
appears on a December
24, 1859 bill. First Lady
Joe Betsy Allred gave
birth to Sam Houston
Allred in this bed on
March 17, 1937.*

T HE SOUTHEAST BEDROOM became the second official state
bedroom in 1982. It was then designated the Sam Houston
Bedroom. The Sam Houston bed and Sam Houston memorabilia
were placed in this room when the Mansion Collection was
moved back into the house following the 1979–1982 restoration-renovation. From the turn of the century, the "Sam Houston Room" had been the southwest bedroom, which today is
known as the Pease Bedroom. The change was made when the
large Pease beds were discovered in the Texas Archives and the
restoration planners realized that the Sam Houston bed fit perfectly between the front windows in the southeast bedroom.

The view from this window is across the front balcony and east to Congress Avenue. The French rosewood side chair by the bed was used in the French Legation in Austin between 1840 and 1842 and was a gift to the Mansion in 1917. The cherry and birch chest of drawers with turned column supports bears the name of its maker, Carey and March, New England, circa 1823. The bronze and crystal lamp is one of a pair acquired by First Lady Janey Briscoe for the state.

The room has been used by First Families as a bedroom, playroom, study, or sitting room. In past years, the room was furnished primarily with personal pieces that the various governors brought with them to the Mansion.

Today, the Sam Houston bed is the central piece in the room and possibly the most historically significant piece relating to the Governor's Mansion. It was thought to have been purchased with state funds during the Houston administration (1859–1861) and to have been in the Mansion since that time. A plaque was placed on it by First Lady Sallie Culberson in 1899 to identify it for future generations. It was handmade, possibly in Texas or Louisiana, for use in the Mansion. Over the years, it has had numerous canopies, curtains, and spreads. Today, it displays a handstitched Lone Star quilt. It has a canopy, dust ruffle, and bedspread of fabric reproducing the famous *Texian Campaigneware* china pattern. This pattern depicts the Mexican War with the United States (1846–1848) in which Texans played a primary role.

Throughout the room are reminders of Sam Houston. Most noteworthy are the photograph of First Lady Margaret Houston,

37

This view of the Sam Houston Bedroom shows a bust of Houston sculpted by Elisabet Ney in 1900. The portrait above the sofa is a hand-painted photograph of Sam Houston. The sofa was machine-made in the American Empire style, circa 1870.

the Elisabet Ney bust, the painted photograph of Sam Houston, and numerous signed documents and letters.

Three important Mansion Collection pieces are now in the Sam Houston Bedroom. The pair of loveseats and the small rosewood side chair by the bed were used in the old French Legation during the days of the Republic of Texas. These pieces were acquired by Austinites when the French ambassador returned home after Texas became a state in 1845. The loveseats and the chair were donated to the Governor's Mansion in the twentieth century.

The Sam Houston Bedroom's restored fireplace is flanked by a pair of French Empire loveseats, or causeuses, *that once belonged to Count A. de Saligny, French Chargé d'Affaires to the Republic of Texas. They were given to the Mansion in 1932 during the Sterling administration (1931–1933). First Lady Maud Sterling stitched the needlepoint cover on the small footstool between the loveseats.*

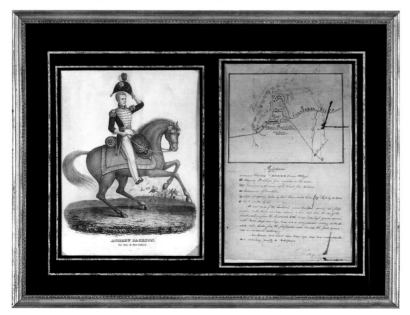

THE BATTLE OF HORSESHOE BEND *is a set of prints which includes rare maps of the battle, a description of the battle, and a lithograph by Kellogg and Company of the victorious general, Andrew Jackson. Twenty-one-year-old Sam Houston was severely wounded in this historic battle against the Creek Indians in Alabama.*

39

Private Quarters

*E*ACH GOVERNOR'S family has had a portion of the house reserved for private family living. In the early days of the Governor's Mansion, this included one or more of the four upstairs bedrooms. The original kitchen wing had a second floor which contained several small bedrooms used primarily as servants' quarters.

As the state grew and public use of the house increased, the family living area and bedroom space became increasingly inadequate, particularly for governors with several children. At the turn of the century, First Lady Lena Sayers furnished the southwest bedroom with the Sam Houston bed and other pieces appropriate for a state bedroom. From that time, at least one upstairs bedroom has been a "public" room.

In 1914, the only major addition to the house was completed, and additional family space became available both upstairs and down. The Family Dining Room, or Conservatory, was added downstairs. More family bedrooms and a porch were added upstairs.

From 1914 to the present, several changes have been made in the Private Quarters of the Mansion. The 1914 upstairs porch has been enclosed. Additional bathrooms have been added, and a kitchen has been included. Several small rooms have been combined to create a large living room and adjoining dining area where the family and friends can gather and entertain. Governor and Mrs. Dolph Briscoe added a large wood-burning fireplace.

The Private Quarters have been decorated at the discretion of the First Families. Historically, this area was furnished with the personal possessions of each governor, leaving it basically empty as each new governor arrived. Today, this situation has changed. With the FRIENDS OF THE GOVERNOR'S MANSION acquisition program, many fine reproduction pieces from downstairs became available for this area. Governors may now enjoy fully furnished Private Quarters. If any governor and his family prefer to bring their furnishings with them, the state pieces in the Private Quarters can be temporarily stored.

The area of the Private Quarters, which today includes the north bedrooms upstairs and the upstairs portion of the 1914 addition, is not on public display at any time. This area makes the Governor's Mansion a true home for the First Family.

The Mansion Gardens

*T*HE GROUNDS of the two-acre Mansion complex are used extensively for entertaining by the governor and first lady. The grounds surround the house and are enclosed with brick and wrought-iron fences.

First Lady Nellie Connally established a formal landscape plan in the 1960s that is still used today. The landscape plan is comprehensive and includes a special entertaining area on the south lawn. The Connally Gardens contain a reflecting pool, a colonial

The east lawn of the Mansion slopes gently to Colorado Street and affords an unobstructed view of the Texas State Capitol across Eleventh Street.

The Mansion Gardens

From the arbor, the gazebo can be seen through the trees and beyond the wrought-iron fence. The fence is topped with five-pointed stars, representing the Lone Star State.

A colonnade marks the entrance to the Connally Gardens.

The Connally Gardens include a reflecting pool, a fountain, and a colonial arbor. Antique cast-iron urns and wrought-iron furniture complement the area.

arbor and colonnade, and brick walkways. The area is used for press conferences, cocktail parties, receptions, and seated dinners. For larger gatherings, tents are often erected on the front lawn of the Mansion.

A replica of the 1870s gazebo, or summerhouse, was constructed on the south lawn during the 1979–1982 restoration-renovation. On the north side of the Mansion, areas have been designated for small herb and vegetable gardens. Alive with seasonal color, the grounds provide a perfect setting for the Greek Revival Mansion.

During the spring and fall, this garden area is used extensively for entertaining. Historic iron fencing, originally on the Capitol grounds, was found in storage at the State Cemetery and installed around the Mansion in the 1960s.

The gazebo, a replica of one built near the same location in the 1870s, is located on the south lawn. The South Entry into the Governor's Mansion, sealed in 1941, has been reopened and restored.

44

Governors' Collection

A FEW SPECIAL ITEMS given to the Mansion by various governors through the years were displayed together for the first time by First Lady Marialice Shivers during the Shivers administration (1949–1957). First Lady Jean Daniel developed the idea of a Governors' Collection and sought at least one gift commemorating each administration. The former governors or their families generously donated mementos to the Governor's Mansion, and Jean Daniel displayed this collection in a bookcase in the Mansion. The Governors' Collection has continued to grow and to occupy a prominent place in the Mansion.

Pease Administrations (1853–1857, 1867–1869)
   1. Shakespeare Book. *Book of colored illustrations given to Lucadia Pease by Governor E. M. Pease, Christmas 1856.*
Runnels Administration (1857–1859)
   2. Colt Pistol. *Belonged to Governor Hardin R. Runnels.*
Houston Administration (1859–1861)
   3. Silver Baby Cup. *Used by the children of General Sam Houston. Inherited by Sam Houston's son, Andrew Jackson Houston, and given to Sam Houston Allred, who was born in the Sam Houston bed in 1937. Presented to the Mansion Collection by Sam Houston Allred in 1961. Engraved: "Houston."*
Houston Administration (1859–1861)
   4. Silver and Crystal Dresser Set. *Rectangular rock crystal dresser set with sterling silver tops, which belonged to Mrs. Sam Houston. Engraved: "H."*

2

3

4

5   6

7

8

12

9

10   11

Clark Administration (1861)

5. Sterling Silver Punch Ladle. *Used during Governor Edward Clark's administration. Engraved: "EMC" in script on the handle.*
6. Sand Shaker. *Barrel-shaped wooden desk piece to absorb ink. Used by Governor Clark at his desk.*

Lubbock Administration (1861–1863)

7. Silver Baby Cup. *Belonging to Governor Francis Lubbock. Engraved: "F.R.L."*

Murrah Administration (1863–1865)

8. Treasury Warrant. *Framed ten dollar treasury note in payment to Governor Pendleton Murrah for military service: "Austin, June 20, 1864, Ten Dollars, No.13647, To P. Murrah."*

Interim Administration (1865)

9. Speech. *Copy of speech delivered by Fletcher S. Stockdale. On cover: "Ex-Governor F. S. Stockdale of Texas Literary Societies of Roanoke College June 15, 1875."*

Hamilton Administration (1865–1866)

10. Coin Silver Spoon. *Belonged to Governor Andrew Hamilton. Unclear engraved initials on back, possibly "AJH."*
11. Silver Napkin Rings. *Two napkin rings in a presentation box engraved "AJH" and "MJH," the initials of Governor Andrew J. Hamilton and First Lady Mary Jane Hamilton.*

Throckmorton Administration (1866–1867)

12. English Silver Teaspoons. *A pair of engraved teaspoons with figural handles used by Governor James W. Throckmorton. Engraved: "T."*

Davis Administration (1870–1874)

13. Union Sword. *Battle sword belonging to Governor Edmund J. Davis.*

Coke Administration (1874–1876)

14. Book. *Personal Reminiscences of General Robert E. Lee, inscribed "Richard Coke, January 25, 1875."*
15. Brass Candlestick. *Graduated ring candleholder used in the Mansion.*

Hubbard Administration (1876–1879)

16. Silver Cake Server. *Presented to Governor Richard B. Hubbard by the government of Japan. Engraved: "J.R.H.," the initials of First Lady Janie Roberts Hubbard.*

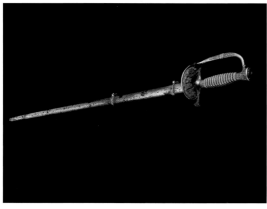

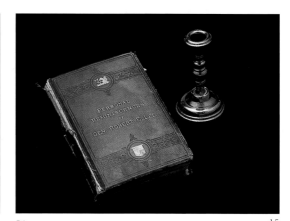

13

14

15

16

17

18

19

20

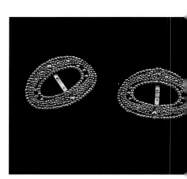

21

Roberts Administration (1879–1883)

17. Cut Class Vinegar Cruet. *From the Governor and Mrs. Oran M. Roberts administration.*

Ireland Administration (1883–1887)

18. Coin Silver Spoon. *Small spoon used by Governor and Mrs. John Ireland in the Mansion. Engraved: "I."*

Ross Administration (1887–1891)

19. Haviland Platter. *A clover-leaf platter, part of the Haviland china pattern from the Lawrence S. Ross administration.*

Hogg Administration (1891–1895)

20. Family Hymnal. *Used by the Hogg family while in the Governor's Mansion. Titled:* Gospel Hymns.

Culberson Administration (1895–1899)

21. Silver Shoe Buckles. *A pair of cut marcasite and silver buckles worn by Mrs. Charles A. Culberson.*

Sayers Administration (1899–1903)

22. Three Books. *Leather-bound book of poems,* Aurora Leigh & Other Poems, *by Elizabeth Barrett Browning, a gift from Governor Sayers to Mrs. Sayers; a second copy of* Aurora Leigh & Other Poems; *and a copy of* Ossian's Poems.

23. Haviland Dessert Set. *Three-piece set of china hand-painted by Mrs. Joseph Sayers.*

23   24   25   26

28   29   30

Lanham Administration (1903–1907)

24. Silver Syrup Pitcher. *Part of flat silver set used by the Lanhams while in the Mansion. Engraved "L 1903" on one side, "Executive Mansion" on the other side.*

25. Inaugural Program. *Leather-bound program from Governor S.W.T. Lanham's Inauguration, dated January 20, 1903.*

Campbell Administration (1907–1911)

26. Engraved Silver Tray. *Presented by "The Women of Austin" in honor of "Mrs. Thomas M. Campbell, Mistress of the Executive Mansion of Texas, 1907–1911."*

Colquitt Administration (1911–1915)

27. Silver Demitasse Spoons. *Five spoons used by Governor and Mrs. Oscar Branch Colquitt in the Mansion. Engraved: "Colquitt" and dated 1912.*

28. Cut Crystal Set. *Place setting of hand-cut crystal, six pieces in the Cosmos pattern used in the Mansion.*

James Ferguson Administration (1915–1917)

29. Engraved Silver Tray. *Old English reproduction silver tray with grape pattern borders, one of a pair. Engraved: "James E. Ferguson, 1915–1917.*

Hobby Administration (1917–1921)

30. Tiffany Silver Bowl. *Footed, sterling silver Tiffany flower bowl purchased in New York by Mrs. Hobby and presented to the Mansion by W. P. Hobby in 1932. Engraved: "In memory of my beloved wife, Willie Cooper Hobby, whose presence graced the Governor's Mansion 1917 to 1921. W. P. Hobby."*

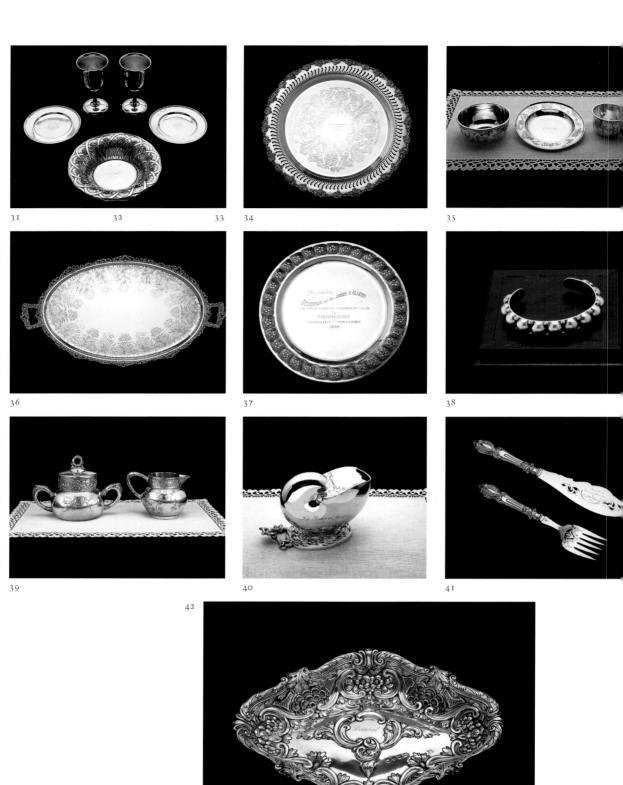

31   32   33   34   35

36   37   38

39   40   41

42

50

Neff Administration (1921–1925)

31. Silver Nut Dish. *Used by Governor and Mrs. Pat Neff. Engraved: "Neff, 1921–1925."*

32. Silver Goblets. *Pair of early Reed and Barton goblets from the Neff administration. Engraved: "M.M.N.," the initials of First Lady Myrtle Mainer Neff.*

33. Bread and Butter Plates. *Set of silver plates from the Neff Estate. Engraved: "M.M.N."*

Miriam Ferguson Administrations (1925–1927, 1933–1935)

34. Silver Tray. *Old English reproduction silver tray with grape pattern used by the Fergusons in the Mansion. Engraved: "Miriam A. Ferguson, 1925–1927, 1933–1935."*

Moody Administration (1927–1931)

35. Silver Baby Set. *Three-piece (plate, cup, and bowl) child's silver set with animal designs. Gift to Dan Moody Jr. in 1929 from the Ladies of the Forty-first Legislature. Engraved: "Dan, Jr."*

Sterling Administration (1931–1933)

36. Engraved Silver Tray. *Presented to Mrs. Ross Sterling by "The Women of Austin." Engraved: "To Mrs. Ross Sterling... Christmas, 1932."*

Allred Administration (1935–1939)

37. Mexican Silver Tray. *A round sterling silver tray which was a gift from Sanborns in Mexico to Governor and Mrs. James Allred. Engraved: "Presented to Governor and Mrs. James V. Allred for the Governor's Mansion of Texas by Sanborns, Mexico City, Monterrey, 1936."*

O'Daniel Administration (1939–1941)

38. Silver Bracelet. *Worn by Molly O'Daniel, daughter of Governor W. Lee O'Daniel, and now mounted in a silver frame.*

Stevenson Administration (1941–1947)

39. Silver Cream and Sugar Set. *Ornate covered sugar bowl and creamer used by Coke Stevenson in the Mansion.*

Jester Administration (1947–1949)

40. Silver Spoon Warmer. *Heavy English silver in conch shell shape. Inscribed: "The Beauford Jesters, 1947."*

Shivers Administration (1949–1957)

41. Silver Fish Servers. *A set of English antique silver fish servers, a fork and a knife purchased during the Allan Shivers administration. Engraved on knife handle: "Presented to Governor's Mansion by Mrs. Allan Shivers, 1962."*

Daniel Administration (1957–1963)

42. Silver Almond Dish. *1835 English silver dish presented by Governor and Mrs. Price Daniel in 1962. Engraved: "Daniel."*

43. Oval Sterling Tray. *Presented to Governor Price Daniel in 1959 by a Mexican delegation on a goodwill tour. Engraved.*

43

45

Connally Administration (1963–1969)

44. Abner Cook Silver Spoon. *Presented to Mrs. John Connally by the heirs of Abner Cook, builder of the Governor's Mansion. Engraved: "A.J.C." on front of spoon. Plaque reads: "Abner Cook's spoon presented to Mrs. John Connally by his granddaughter, 1963."*

Smith Administration (1969–1973)

45. Carved Mockingbird. *Wooden mockingbird carved by James Eddleman and presented by the Preston Smiths to the Mansion to commemorate the state bird.*

Clements Administration (1979–1983, 1987–1991)

46. Boehm American Eagle. *Porcelain eagle presented by Governor and Mrs. William P. Clements, Jr.*

White Administration (1983–1991)

47. Silver Covered Cup. *Presented by Governor and Mrs. Mark White. Engraved: "Governor Mark White 1983–1987."*

Richards Administration (1991–1995)

48. Mexican Silver Necklace and Earrings. *Jewelry presented by Governor Ann Richards.*

49. Pewter Plaque. *Plaque identifying the Governors' Collection. Engraved.*

44

46

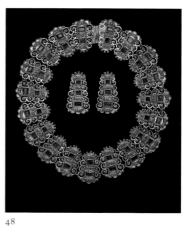

48

47

49

50

51

53

52

53

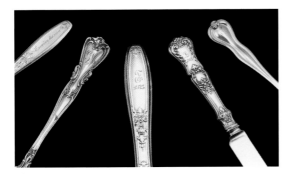

54

55

Governors' Mementos and Gifts Throughout the Mansion

50. Pease Cane (in the Pease Bedroom). *Hand-carved elephant's head cane given to Elisha Marshall Pease in 1880. Donated by Governor and Mrs. Allan Shivers. Presented to Governor and Mrs. William P. Clements, Jr. and Friends of the Governor's Mansion in 1982 in celebration of the completed restoration project. Engraved.*

51. Shadowbox (in the Pease Bedroom). *Used to display gifts given to E. M. Pease by Sam Houston. Contains a wooden snuffbox whittled by Sam Houston and a small English tea caddy-style black box probably used for jewelry.*

52. Original Photograph of the Governor's Mansion (in the Pease Bedroom). *From the Davis administration (1870–1874). Handwritten on back: "We arrived in Austin, and went to the 'Gov. Mansion,' March 17th (Thursday) at 6 P.M. from Corpus Christi, Texas 1870."*

53. Large Sheffield Silver Tray (in the Conservatory). *Given to the Mansion by Governor and Mrs. Allan Shivers when they left the Mansion in January 1957. Engraved.*

54. Silver Flatware (in the Entry Hall). *A collection of the flatware patterns used in the Mansion during the Lanham, Colquitt, Ferguson, Stevenson, and Jester administrations.*

55. Empire Mantel Lamp (in the Small Parlor). *One of a set of three ornate Empire lamps with prisms and frosted etched shades purchased and given to the Mansion by Mrs. Dan Moody in 1939.*

PART TWO

The Restoration

On April 1, 1982, Bill and Rita Clements officially reopened the Mansion with a press conference and tour. Daily public tours resumed on April 14.

1st floor 1856

G OVERNOR AND MRS. WILLIAM P. CLEMENTS, JR. realized shortly after his election in November of 1978 that the Texas Governor's Mansion, their future home, was in desperate need of attention. Paint was peeling, carpets were stained, the kitchen facilities were inadequate, and no satisfactory restroom facilities existed for the thousands of guests who visit in the home each year. Every room in the Governor's Mansion needed repairs, if not major renovation.

Both Governor and Mrs. Clements had been involved in historic preservation projects. In 1970, Bill Clements had restored the Cumberland Public School on the edge of downtown Dallas and made it the corporate headquarters for Sedco, the company he founded in January of 1947. That project has served as a model, demonstrating that innovative use of historic buildings can work successfully.

Rita Clements had also been active in historic preservation, most significantly as a member, since 1975, of the Fine Arts Committee of the State Department Reception Rooms. She became more knowledgeable of nineteenth-century American antiques and met dealers in this country that have access to fine period furniture. Through her involvement with the State Department, as well as with the White House, she learned what was required to organize and fund a major restoration effort.

By the time of the January inauguration, Bill and Rita Clements had made the Texas Governor's Mansion one of their major priorities. They had concluded that either the Mansion would have to be totally renovated to provide for appropriate entertaining and comfortable living or it should become a museum, with the state providing a new home for the governor. With their love of history, they preferred the former but felt the decision was not theirs to make. Governor Clements asked the legislature to appoint a committee to study the options, make an official recommendation, and estimate the cost of that recommendation. By Senate Resolution No. 23, the Sixty-sixth Legislature created a study committee comprised of Representatives Bob Davis and Pete Laney, Senators Bill Braecklein and Tom Creighton, and two citizen members appointed by Governor Clements. Appointed were former First Lady Mrs. Price Daniel, Sr. and Mrs. H. Ross Perot, a member of the Texas Commission on the Arts. Jean Daniel, the great-great-granddaughter of another Mansion resident, Sam Houston, was chosen as chairperson of this study committee.

The committee accepted Dallas architect Jim Hendricks of the Dallas firm of Burson, Hendricks, and Walls as the project

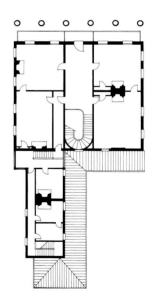

2nd floor 1856

1st floor   1914

architect. Governor and Mrs. Clements encouraged this choice, based on Mr. Hendricks's work as one of the architects for the Cumberland School project ten years earlier.

The study committee quickly decided in favor of preserving the 123-year-old house as the official residence. They worked with restoration architect Jim Hendricks to review the project needs and to estimate costs. Both the Texas Commission on the Arts and the State Purchasing and General Services Commission were brought in to help finalize plans. They then asked the Sixty-sixth Legislature for $1,000,000 to structurally restore the historic home. The legislature appropriated the money before it adjourned May 28, 1979.

Governor and Mrs. Clements knew that the state appropriation was only the beginning. Private support and funding would be needed for the complete restoration and renovation of the Governor's Mansion, both inside and out. Never before had sufficient funding been available for the Mansion. To raise the necessary funds for appropriate furnishings and interior decoration, they formed the organization FRIENDS OF THE GOVERNOR'S MANSION.

FRIENDS OF THE GOVERNOR'S MANSION is a Texas nonprofit corporation, chartered in November of 1979 for the benefit of the Governor's Mansion in Austin, Texas. It was and is committed to maintaining and preserving the historical and cultural significance of this home and its contents.

Under the direction of its statewide Board of Directors headed by the late Mr. Ashley Priddy, FRIENDS was incorporated to receive private funding to form a collection of museum-quality, nineteenth-century American and Texas furnishings and works of art to complement and enhance the existing Mansion Collection. Governor and Mrs. Clements were active participants in contacting people and helping to raise over $3,000,000 for the Mansion project. The long-term goals of FRIENDS OF THE GOVERNOR'S MANSION were to acquire a museum-quality collection of furniture, restore items in the state-owned Mansion Collection, inform and educate the public, enhance the landscaping of the grounds, and maintain a formal curating system to preserve the Mansion Collection.

An Acquisitions Committee was responsible for the selection and proposed placement of the newly acquired collection. Several members of this committee also sat on the Mansion Subcommittee of the Texas Commission on the Arts, whose final approval had to be given to any acquisition in the Mansion Collection. Through this process, all changes in the collection were approved by the Acquisitions Committee of FRIENDS, the Board of Directors of FRIENDS, and the Texas Commission on the Arts and its Mansion Subcommittee.

Several individuals served as advisors in the 1979–1982 period. The Houston Museum of Fine Arts loaned its associate director David Warren to the project. He was a former curator of Bayou Bend, the Houston home of Miss Ima Hogg, and he shared his knowledge of nineteenth-century American furniture. Clement Conger, curator of the White House and State Department Reception Rooms, generously advised FRIENDS on various aspects of the project. Dallas designers Jed Mace and Tom Sellman worked on the project from start to finish. Mr. Mace suggested placement of items already in the collection, recommended acquisitions based on space and functional needs, and coordinated choices of colors, fabrics, and area rugs. Governor and Mrs. Clements served as advisory members of the FRIENDS board. First Lady Rita Clements became actively involved in all aspects of the Mansion project.

No plans survived from the 1854–1856 construction of the house, and plans from the 1914 addition period were not complete. Architect Hendricks, in addition to his work on the project, made measured sets of drawings of the house as it might have appeared in 1856 and in 1914, as it existed in 1979 before the restoration-renovation, and as it would be when the project was complete. All the sets of measured plans were donated to the Texas State Archives.

In 1979, contractors submitted bids to the state, and the firm of Lawless and Alford gave the low bid. They were awarded the contract to begin work in March of 1980. The Austin architectural firm of Wilson, Stoeltje, Martin, Inc. was hired to assist Burson, Hendricks, and Walls as "Clerk of the Works" at the site once the work was underway. They were to oversee the project on a day-to-day basis and help with alterations as work progressed.

In the summer of 1979, Governor and Mrs. Bill Clements moved out of the Mansion. They moved a portion of the Mansion Collection to an apartment in the Cambridge Tower in Austin.

As the Mansion was emptied, each item was inventoried. This process began what was to become the first formal curating system for the state-owned Mansion Collection. Curating sheets were completed on each piece, giving a full description, a current appraisal, and the location of the piece in 1979. Most important, each item was evaluated as to its historic significance. An unpublished listing in book form of the Mansion contents during the late 1950s had been compiled by First Lady Jean Daniel. Additional records kept by Mrs. Daniel and Austin writer Dorothy Blodgett provided invaluable information for the Mansion project.

Furniture that was not moved into the apartment went either to storage or to restoration experts for repair and refinishing. Items of particular historic or aesthetic value such as the Sam

2nd floor 1914

1st floor   1979

2nd floor   1979

Houston bed, gifts from Miss Ima Hogg, paintings, and silver were the first to be placed in the new decorative plans. A few items that the Texas Commission on the Arts felt should be retained in the Mansion Collection but which did not fit into the room plans were kept in storage for future use.

Several historically significant additions to the Mansion Collection resulted in the designation of a second official state bedroom. First Lady Rita Clements arranged for the transfer of the Pease four-poster beds from the Texas State Archives. The southwest bedroom was designated the Pease Bedroom in honor of the Mansion's first residents. Governor Pease's desk was returned to the Mansion from the Capitol and restored along with the beds. The Pease portraits were then donated to FRIENDS OF THE GOVERNOR'S MANSION by the Pease descendants and were hung in the room after extensive restoration work was completed at the Kimbell Art Museum. In 1982, Governor and Mrs. Allan Shivers gave FRIENDS a magnificent carved cane that had belonged to Elisha Marshall Pease.

The project included many changes that restored the architectural details of the original 1856 house. All of the nine fireplaces that had been a part of the original house were restored to working order. Although all had originally been wood burning, today only those in the Large Parlor, Small Parlor, and Library are wood burning. The remaining six are equipped only for coal. This required rebuilding the chimneys, all of which had been removed during the Shivers administration because of the fire hazard caused by the degeneration of the interior bricks. The fireboxes and linings were reworked, and most of the mantels were restored to reflect the styling of the 1856 Library mantel which was still in place.

The front porch was returned to its original character by replacing the existing red brick with wood on both the porch and the steps. The Texas Historical Foundation provided guidance and funding to construct a replica of the 1870s gazebo on the south lawn.

The original south entrance was restored, replacing the very small powder room that had been built in 1941 during the Stevenson administration. The flooring replicated the wideplank pine flooring that was used in the original construction. Edgegrained, seasoned pine boards were required for this process; a nationwide search was successful in providing just enough old lumber to complete the flooring in the public rooms, including the Upstairs Hall and the two state bedrooms. The stairwell window was returned to its original design and was shuttered to give the appearance of the exterior window that it had been in 1856.

Texans had strong feelings that they expressed when it was suggested that the Mansion might not be painted white but a light tan or buff color. Research indicates that the Mansion's buff-colored brick was first painted in the 1870s in an attempt to halt further deterioration of the natural brick. The paint color approximated the natural light buff color of the brick. It was not until sometime in the early twentieth century that the Mansion was first painted white.

In addition to the aesthetic demands of historic preservation, the house desperately needed some practical changes. The interior walls were stripped down as far as possible and patched where necessary. A canvas wallcovering was then placed over the walls to protect the old plaster and create a uniform appearance. Supports were checked and rebraced in a number of places where structural alignment was required. Sagging floor joists were reworked in several rooms. The foundation was discovered to be sound and stable, having been worked on extensively during the Daniel administration (1957–1963). It required only minor adjustments to assure structural integrity for the future.

The Mansion's almost flat roof required work, as it had with regularity during the history of the house. It was completely replaced to protect the interior restoration.

The plumbing was checked and repaired where necessary. New plumbing fixtures were installed throughout the house. The electricity was also checked and upgraded. The air conditioning and heating systems were examined. The security and fire systems were modernized with a grant from the Criminal Justice Division of the governor's office.

1st floor   1982

The most significant practical changes were the expansion of the kitchen facilities and the additions of a powder room and a men's room off the Back Entry. The new areas were created from a combination of the 1914 butler's pantry, kitchen, storage area, and security station. Ceilings were raised throughout this back portion of the house. This space was redesigned to provide for the bathrooms, a coat closet area, and a greatly expanded kitchen that could accommodate large appliances needed to service Mansion parties and dinners.

Some changes were made that created needed space in the Private Quarters and the office areas in the Carriage House. The Private Quarters were redesigned for better use, opening up small areas and creating more usable space. Floors were brought up to one level. The large red brick fireplace and wall that the Briscoes had built was paneled. Fine quality reproduction furnishings which had been used in the public areas of the Mansion in the past were reupholstered and used to furnish the Private Quarters. Governors and first ladies would no longer have to bring in their own furniture to live comfortably in the Mansion.

The Carriage House was rearranged and upgraded inside to better accommodate security and staff offices on the second floor. On the first floor, a storage area was created and a bathroom

2nd floor   1982

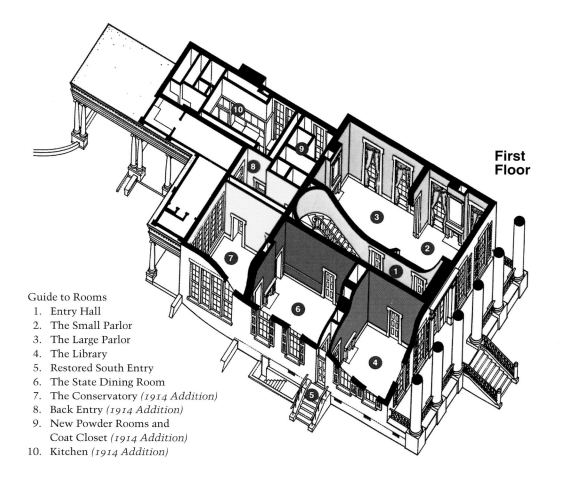

First Floor

Guide to Rooms
 1. Entry Hall
 2. The Small Parlor
 3. The Large Parlor
 4. The Library
 5. Restored South Entry
 6. The State Dining Room
 7. The Conservatory *(1914 Addition)*
 8. Back Entry *(1914 Addition)*
 9. New Powder Rooms and
      Coat Closet *(1914 Addition)*
10. Kitchen *(1914 Addition)*

facility for the handicapped was added in the renovated Carriage House. The exterior of the Carriage House was changed slightly for aesthetic reasons.

The porte cochere was widened to better accommodate modern vehicles. It was completely redesigned with new Greek columns to better suit the Mansion's architectural design and to recapture the look of 1914 photographs.

Finally, the gardens were upgraded and replanted, making every effort to retain the original character of the Connally landscape plan. Lamberts, Inc. updated the landscape plan they had done for Governor and Mrs. John Connally in the 1960s. The sprinkler system was upgraded, and exterior lighting was redesigned by John Watson of Dallas. Trees were pruned, new trees were planted, and beds were prepared for new plants. Paint was stripped from the red brick wall surrounding the grounds, and a French drain system was built to ensure that a new coat of white paint would adhere.

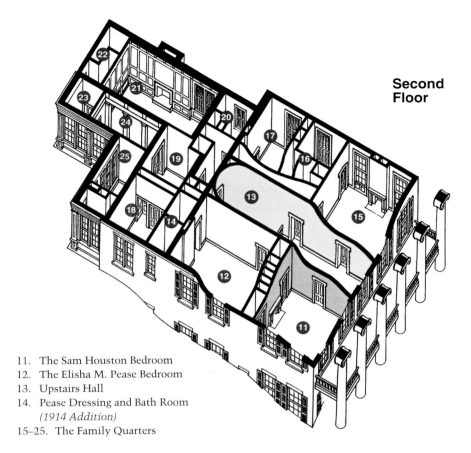

Second Floor

11. The Sam Houston Bedroom
12. The Elisha M. Pease Bedroom
13. Upstairs Hall
14. Pease Dressing and Bath Room
       (1914 Addition)
15–25. The Family Quarters

    In January of 1982, Governor and Mrs. Clements moved back into the house, but it took another three months before the restoration-renovation project was completed. When they moved the first furniture from storage and brought the furniture from the Cambridge Tower in early January, there were still no rugs, draperies, or pictures on the walls. Rooms were not complete; workmen putting on the finishing touches were in every room of the house until the official opening in April. The project that was to take one year had taken almost three.

    When the Mansion reopened to the public on April 14, 1982, it was complete inside and out for the first time in its history. Governor and Mrs. Clements held a press conference on the Mansion steps to introduce the press and the public to the newly renovated home.

    With the restoration-renovation project complete, FRIENDS was charged with informing the people of Texas about the Governor's Mansion. A Mansion brochure is available for use at the Mansion during special tours. A twenty-five minute documentary,

The Texas Governor's Mansion, was produced in 1993 in conjunction with KLRU, the public television station in Austin, and made available to the public and Texas schools. A committee of FRIENDS, Docents of the Governor's Mansion, is available to guide special tours through the house and is trained in the history of the house and the Mansion Collection. The Mansion guidebook is funded and published by FRIENDS OF THE GOVERNOR'S MANSION.

At the January 11, 1983, board meeting, FRIENDS set aside $500,000 as a permanent endowment fund to maintain the collection for the benefit of future residents and all Texans. FRIENDS has retained title to the items acquired during the restoration-renovation and will continue to use the endowment fund income to insure, repair, restore, and curate the Mansion Collection. With continued support from the state and private donors, the Governor's Mansion can be maintained for the enjoyment of all Texans.

PART THREE

An Historic Perspective

Courtyard, Spanish Governor's Palace, San Antonio.

Sam Houston's residence in Houston during his first term as president of the Republic of Texas (1837–1838).

From the Beginning:
Log Cabin to Mansion

Joe Frantz

Professor of History
University of Texas at Austin

WHEN IN THE DAWN of leadership, tribal leaders, lords and nobles, and finally princes and kings began to emerge, it became accepted that the leader would have superior housing. Whatever his title, his elevated status among the people was reflected in his housing. In early days, the tribal leaders might have no more than an extra elk's tooth over their tent. The presence of some insignia was the first indication that here lived persons of distinction.

In time, lords of the manor became established, and their very titles showed their power and wealth. They could command soldiers, workers, and even slaves. They had the finest houses because they had amassed the most of the world's goods in their areas. Lesser people lived in the shadow of the manor houses, worked, and paid tithes and taxes to maintain their lords. They fought when ordered to and were willing to give up their lives for their lord and prince and his way of life. They could forget their own miserable lodgings in the knowledge that their ruler lived in a style beyond their dreams.

Throughout the long course of history, the idea that the people of the state or nation should provide residences for their leaders gradually became established—whether those leaders were temporary or permanent or whether they were imposed, elected, or inherited. England built its Buckingham and Windsor palaces. France had its Versailles. Germany was dotted with castles belonging to the heads of its principalities. Most of the nations of the world have demonstrated this principle of providing homes for their leaders.

Spanish Texas

The growth of the idea into a tradition can be traced across Europe and to the early days of America, to the 1600s when Spanish explorers claimed the vast lands known later as Mexico and Texas. Spain ruled these lands for three hundred years, building missions and forts, then establishing provincial capitals. In these capitals, residences were built for the Spanish governors of the provinces.

The governors of Coahuila, a northern province including the lands of Texas, had lived in a number of temporary capitals.

It was at Bexar (now San Antonio) that the Spanish Governor's Palace (now a museum) was built before 1749. It might be said, in a historic sense, that the Spanish Governor's Palace was a forerunner of today's Texas Governor's Mansion.

In typical Spanish style, the Governor's Palace fronted directly onto the street on Military Plaza. Its yards and gardens were in the back of the building. The garden remains a serene spot in the center of busy San Antonio, a romantic area with its overhanging trees, clusters of flowers and vines, and its many stone benches. In this garden over a century and a half ago, James Bowie, later a hero of the Alamo, came to call upon Ursula María Veramendi, daughter of the vice-governor. Señor Juan Martín Veramendi and his family were living in the Palace in the absence of the governor. This was one of those periods when the seat of government was moved to Saltillo or Monclova, Mexico, and the vice-governor was left to govern the province. And in March 1831, James Bowie and Ursula Veramendi were married.

The Governor's Palace is a fine example of Spanish construction and design. Its walls were built of hand-formed bricks, as were those of the Greek Revival Mansion built in Austin a century later. The Palace walls were lined with plaster or mortar, and some were painted pastel green or blue. Period artifacts, such as square-cut nails, heavy spikes, and brass stripping can be seen.

The Spanish Governor's Palace was a crumbling ruin when the city of San Antonio purchased it in 1929 and began its reconstruction. Later, the United States Department of the Interior designated it as a National Historic Landmark.

The last governor appointed by Spain for its northern province of Coahuila was Antonio Martínez. He lived in the Palace while his Spanish compatriots were being driven out of Mexico. That country was in a state of rebellion against Spain. In the meantime, Moses Austin and his friend and servant, Richmond, came to San Antonio and appealed to Governor Martínez to permit Americans to establish colonies in Texas. The governor and the Spanish officials still in Mexico approved the colonization petition in 1821. Moses Austin died soon after, and it was his son, Stephen Fuller Austin, who brought the settlers, called the "Old Three Hundred," into Texas. But Stephen Fuller Austin did not have a palace or a mansion built for him. Soon after he established the colony located on a bend of the Colorado River and later named San Felipe, he wrote his mother and sister to join him and live in a house "plain and pretty much like the rest of our neighbors. We are all poor in this country and therefore all on an equality and so long as this continues we shall all go on well and harmoniously as regards good neighbors." The house was a log cabin.

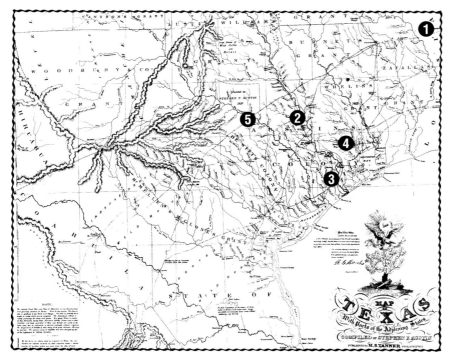

Map of Texas in 1837.
Capitals are:
1. Los Adaes
2. Washington-on-the-Brazos
3. Columbia
4. Houston
5. Austin

The Capitals of Texas

The colony of San Felipe did not become a capital of Texas. An earlier Spanish settlement named Los Adaes may be called the "first capital of Texas." The provincial government of Spanish leaders was established there in the mid-1700s in a fort built near present-day Robeline, Louisiana. This capital of Texas was surrounded by a pointed-log stockade. Los Adaes remained the capital for fifty years (1722–1772).

In the late 1700s, French settlements threatened Spanish dominion in Texas. Earlier, French explorers had raised the flag of France over Texas and lands of the Mississippi River. But Spanish rule prevailed—until Mexico gained independence from Spain in 1821. Texas was then made a part of the Republic of Mexico.

After Texas became independent in 1836, it moved the capital with such frequency that to trace the changes becomes confusing. Fifteen years after the American colonies were first established at San Felipe, the time had come for Texas to have its own capital.

In March 1836, Washington-on-the-Brazos was named the capital of the new and independent Republic of Texas. Government leaders met in a crude frame house with cotton cloth stretched across its windows in lieu of glass. The Republic was so poor that it tried to take over a saloon for the meeting place of the house of representatives; a loft above a gambling house was finally rented. For the senate, the government found a floor above a grocery store. Paying even a three-dollar-a-week rent proved an

69

almost insurmountable task for the new government. Providing an executive mansion was out of the question.

The capital was moved to Columbia in October 1836. There, the house for President Sam Houston was left unfinished and mostly unfurnished. When General Felix Huston came to visit the Republic of Texas' chief executive, Houston gave his guest his bed while he, the president, slept on the floor.

The capital was moved again. In December 1836, the government moved to Houston. For the first time, the Capitol was a "proper," two-story frame building. But the president lived in what has been described as a "mean shack."

In 1839, the capital was established in the little community of Waterloo, later renamed Austin. The government of the Texas Republic appointed Edwin Waller to construct a Capitol on the site named for the Father of Texas. Seventeen years later, now a member of the United States, Texas would build a Governor's Mansion.

The Capital at Austin

In the 1830s when Sam Houston first came to Austin, he stayed at Bullock's Hotel. Meanwhile, a two-story frame house was being jerry-built for the president's occupancy. Called the "White House," it briefly became the town's social center, a place for balls and receptions for the dignitaries who came to Austin. Not many outsiders arrived, for a trip from Houston required twenty-five days each way. Railroads later would be built between the two cities, and connections were made halfway, at Brenham and Columbus. Even when those two towns were reached, it still required ten hours to Houston or Austin. If rains were persistent, Austin might be isolated from stage coaches and wagons for days or weeks. The roads south to San Antonio were poor, while little reason existed for traveling north from the capital.

The town of Austin sat isolated on the upper frontier of Texas. Fear of a Mexican invasion and the uncertainty of its remaining the capital dropped the population from 856 inhabitants in 1840 to 659 a decade later.

The people of Austin persisted in efforts to keep the capital. During his second administration as president, Sam Houston tried to remove the archives to Houston by way of Washington-on-the-Brazos. Excitement took over the town as a boarding-house mistress, noticing the wagons stealing away with the young nation's historic papers, lighted a nearby cannon and shot a warning salvo. The six-pounders hit the new Land Office building and brought out the townspeople. They chased the wagons until daylight and turned them back. The incident made a heroine of Mrs. Angelina Ebberly and gave the small town an interesting story.

It is not difficult to imagine Texas in the mid-1800s. The leaders gathered at log hotels such as Bullock's (which stood on the southeast corner of Sixth Street and Congress Avenue), at various saloons, or in the yard in front of the Treasury building, discussing the affairs of state. Perhaps Mirabeau B. Lamar, the second president of the Republic of Texas, debated there with Sam Houston, the first and the third president. Other leaders in a discussion might have been Governors J. Pinckney Henderson, George Wood, and Peter Hansborough Bell. Former cabinet officers and renowned Texas Rangers Ben and Henry McCulloch, Jack Hays, and Edward Burleson, Jr. must have met and talked in the shade of the trees around the frame Texas state buildings. One of the recurring topics was undoubtedly the need for a permanent executive mansion to replace the quickly built wooden home for the president of the Republic. Later, others would gather on the steps of the 1853 capitol.

On Austin's original plat, space had been set aside for a permanent executive house on a site where the Old Land Office now stands. Some of the leaders, including state Senator and future Governor Elisha Marshall Pease and Mrs. Pease, felt that a better site was a small area to the west. Here on a small hill, future governors could live nearby but not on the main Capitol grounds. The Governor's Mansion has dominated this hill since 1856, when the home was finished.

The old "White House," or "President's House," in Austin fell into disrepair in the mid-1800s and was eventually torn

This drawing was done in 1840, showing Austin, The Seat of Texas Government. The President's House is drawn in detail on the left and shown in its location on the right.

71

Bullock's Hotel at 6th and Congress was a popular hotel and boarding house for the early officeholders when they came to Austin on state business. The old Texas Capitol is visible at the end of Congress Avenue.

down. The other early wooden buildings are gone, those that housed the government of first the Republic and then the State of Texas. Their losses make the Texas Governor's Mansion especially significant. It is still with us, a monument not only to all the governors and their families, but also to the life and times of the many men and women who built our state.

The Mansion stands for the contributions of many peoples, the Spanish, the French, the Mexican, the American settlers, the blacks, and those who came from foreign shores to live in the land of the Tejas.

The Governor's Mansion stands for those long-ago days when history was in the making. That was the beginning. The road of history led from fortress homes at Los Adaes, from log cabins at San Felipe, from crude frame houses in early capitals, to Bullock's Hotel and a group of citizens planning a mansion in Austin in the mid-nineteenth century.

By tracing the path of history, we realize the Governor's Mansion is a culmination of all the efforts to build both a house and a state. In 1854 when construction began, the planners and builders not only built a governor's home, they built a tradition.

An Architect's View of the Governor's Mansion

Drury Blakeley Alexander

Meadows Foundation Professor of Architecture
University of Texas at Austin

T HE GOVERNOR'S MANSION OF TEXAS is the state's premier example of the Greek Revival style of the mid-nineteenth century. The Mansion was completed only seventeen years after the founding of Austin, and the history of its construction and preservation is an interesting one.

Austin at the time the Mansion was built was still a small frontier community. Mirabeau B. Lamar, the second president of the Republic of Texas, had chosen the site of the capital city, and he took an active role in its planning. The plan, as laid out by Edwin Waller, featured a spacious main street which ran from the Colorado River up to the site for the capitol.

In addition to providing a site for the capitol, a lot was set aside for the president's house. The first structures built to house the government and the president were simple wood buildings and were not intended to be permanent accommodations. By 1854, the Republic of Texas had become, by annexation, the State of Texas; and a masonry capitol building had been built on Capitol Square at the head of Congress Avenue. It was time to consider the building of an executive home befitting a state of the United States.

This 1840 drawing shows Austin as laid out by Edwin Waller. The two-story President's House is visible on the east, and the first capitol is visible on the west side of Congress Avenue.

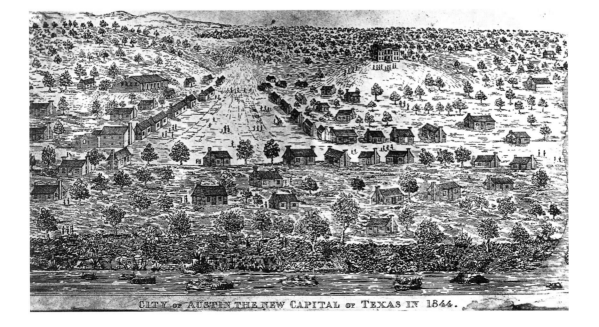

CITY OF AUSTIN THE NEW CAPITAL OF TEXAS IN 1844.

The legislature appropriated $14,500 for a governor's house and $2,500 for furnishings. A committee, consisting of Governor Elisha Marshall Pease and two other commissioners, James H. Raymond and James Shaw, was named to furnish plans and to oversee the building. These three men, all prominent in the political and financial affairs of the state, played an important role in the building of the Mansion.

Governor Pease, born in 1812 in Enfield, Connecticut, came to Texas by way of New Orleans and settled in Bastrop in 1835. He took part in the Texas Revolution and in the Constitutional Convention which followed. After studying law, he held various offices, serving in the house of representatives and in the senate before becoming governor in 1853.

James B. Shaw was born in Ireland about 1799 and graduated from the University of Dublin before immigrating to the United States, settling temporarily in New Orleans. He came to Texas in 1837 and by 1839 was elected to the office of state comptroller, a position which he held until 1859.

The other commissioner, James H. Raymond, was born in Washington County, New York, in 1817. He arrived in Texas in 1840 and, after holding several positions in the government, became treasurer of the state in 1846.

These three men who were to oversee the building of the Mansion were not frontiersmen. They were educated and well traveled, and they had been exposed to the current architectural styles of the major cities of this country. They were not, it should be noted, from the South. Only the year before, Shaw and Raymond had employed the local master builder, Abner Cook, to build what were most likely the finest homes in Austin. The third member of the committee, Governor Pease, would become the first occupant of the Mansion and would later purchase James Shaw's house. Men in their position would undoubtedly expect an executive mansion to be more imposing than their own homes.

Although there is no documentary evidence, Abner Cook is most likely responsible for the design of the Mansion. A man by the name of Richard Payne was paid $100 by Cook for plans for the Texas Governor's Mansion, and it was presumably on the basis of these plans that the first bids were submitted. These bids turned out to be so much higher than the legislative appropriation that the Mansion committee decided to reduce the size of the building in an effort to meet the $14,500 limit. This would suggest that a new set of plans, whether by Payne or someone else, was put out for a second bidding. This time Abner Cook was the low bidder and, on the basis of his bid of $14,500, was awarded the building contract.

It is regrettable that neither the original nor the revised plans exist. However, it is recorded that in revising the original plans,

Master builder Abner Cook.

Hendricks' measured drawing of the proposed wings.

the committee eliminated two side wings and the fencing and also reduced the depth of the house from fifty to forty-five feet. (The house, as built, however, measures nearly sixty feet square, not counting the later additions of the kitchen wing and Conservatory.) The mention of wings on the Mansion is curious in that such elements are not very often found on Greek Revival houses, and it brings up the question of what houses may have influenced the design.

Because so little is known about Richard Payne, the man who was paid for the first plans, it is not possible to speculate on what buildings he may have seen or where he may have traveled before his work on the Mansion. Payne, together with James Phillips, bought the "Old Capitol," which would have been the wooden temporary one, in 1858, and used the material in building the market house. This indicates that he was involved in construction, but he is not mentioned as a builder or architect in connection with any other buildings in Austin, either before the Governor's Mansion was built or after. Without records to indicate his role, the question is raised whether Richard Payne was a designer or merely a draftsman who furnished the drawings for the builder.

Of Abner Cook, more is known. He was born in Salisbury, North Carolina, in 1814. At the age of twenty-one, he left North

75

Carolina for Georgia. He is thought to have lived in Macon, Georgia, for two years before moving to Nashville, Tennessee. Nashville in 1837 must have been a stimulating place for a young man starting his career in building. The Greek Revival style which Cook was to introduce in Austin had only recently made its appearance in Nashville with the building of the Presbyterian Church in 1833, noted for its handsome Doric Temple facade.

Although numerous other Greek Revival buildings were constructed during and before Cook's stay in Nashville, he left the city before the capitol, its most famous building in that style, was built by one of the nation's leading Greek Revival architects, William Strickland. It is unlikely that Cook ever met Strickland, a Philadelphia architect, who came to Nashville to build the capitol about 1844, five years after Cook had moved to Austin.

In the nineteenth century, the usual practice for one interested in becoming a builder was to be apprenticed to a master builder for a number of years while learning the craft and techniques of building. Young Abner Cook may have begun his apprenticeship in North Carolina or Georgia. It is also possible that he became an apprentice in Nashville to the builders Joseph Reiff and William C. Hume, one of the leading building partnerships in Nashville. In 1837, only a year before Cook arrived in Nashville, Reiff and Hume had completed the rebuilding of Andrew Jackson's home, the Hermitage, which had been destroyed by fire.

The Hermitage was an innovative and influential design in the Greek Revival style. The front of the house is dominated by a porch composed of six giant columns supporting an entablature of considerable depth. This entablature rises above and completely hides the gable of the roof, resulting in a strong horizontal line for the roof above the colonnade. On each side of the porch, and in line with it, are two small, one-story wings which are rarely found on Greek Revival houses. It is inconceivable that Cook would not have seen such an important house as the Hermitage while he was in Nashville and that he was not impressed by it. The unusual wing design of the Hermitage may well have inspired Cook in his planning for the Texas Governor's Mansion.

Abner Cook arrived in Austin in 1839, the year that the city was founded. For the next forty-five years, Cook participated in the growth of Austin by contributing many fine buildings, some of which we still enjoy today. For some time after his arrival, his building efforts were limited to the simplest and most practical of frame structures which had to be erected as quickly as possible in order to house families, businesses, and public offices for the newly established capital. By 1855, Abner Cook was a master builder and prominent citizen. He had served as an alderman of the city and was one of the organizers of the First Presbyterian Church. He was one of the contractors of the "Old Capitol" of 1853 and had finished, only the previous year, fine residences for two of the commissioners on the Governor's Mansion Committee, Shaw and Raymond.

The Greek Revival style, as it appeared in Austin, was the contribution of Abner Cook. The design first appeared in a number of residences that Cook built for the city's leading citizens. In addition to the two mentioned for Shaw (Woodlawn) and Raymond, Cook built large Greek Revival homes for John M. Swisher (Sweetbrush), Mrs. Reuben Runner (the Chandler-Shelley House), and Washington L. Hill (the Neill-Cochran House). Four of these houses, including the Governor's Mansion, still exist on their original sites, and one has been moved and re-erected. These houses constitute the finest Greek Revival houses in the city, and possibly in the state.

While not all of these houses in Austin can be documented as having been built by Cook, they are so closely related in style, detail, and quality that there is little reason to doubt his authorship. All had two-story, central hall plans with four rooms on

Woodlawn

Raymond House

Swisher House

Neill-Cochran House

each floor. Two had Doric porticos, and four had Ionic. The two characteristic features which serve to identify Abner Cook's large houses in the Greek Revival style are the horizontal lines of the roof (without pediment or gable) and the elegantly crafted balcony railing in the "X-and-stick" pattern. Of these houses, only the Swisher house had a portico which did not extend the entire width of the house; it had a central portico which featured paired Ionic columns to either side of the entrance door. This house was disassembled and rebuilt on another site in Austin by the late Dr. and Mrs. Z.T. Scott. It was given by the Scott family to the University of Texas, but the house later became a private residence.

The usual procedure for building a fine home in the mid- nineteenth century was for the owner and builder to consult one of the architectural pattern books or builder's handbooks available at the time. The two most popular authors were Asher Benjamin and Minard LaFever who published numerous titles, including *The American Builder's Companion* and *The Modern Builder*, respectively. In these handbooks, the plans for these houses rarely varied from a central hall with two rooms on either side. Symmetry was taken for granted; the door must be in the center, and windows must be equal in number and equally spaced on either side. The order of the columns, whether Doric or Ionic, and such details as mantels, newel posts, and balusters for the stairs and door trim would be selected from the handbooks. Within such limits, the builder and owner would find many ways to achieve originality and uniqueness, as these Austin houses attest.

As befits its purpose, the Governor's Mansion is the grandest of the Greek Revival mansions in Austin. Its thirty-foot columns support a six-foot entablature which conceals the very low hipped roof, giving the appearance of a flat roof. The porch extends the full fifty-eight-foot width of the front of the house and features six great Ionic columns. These columns, with their beautifully executed Greek Ionic capitals, are the most impressive feature of the house. The fluted shafts were made by joining staves with splines, somewhat as a barrel is made. The staves, or boards, are probably of Bastrop pine and were fluted by planing by hand. As the columns are tapered, each board tapers, as do the flutes in each board. Disklike spacers are placed intermittently inside the columns to add stiffness and to maintain the correct taper. These columns could only have been built by a very skilled and experienced builder. The capitals are so well crafted that they may have been ordered from an architectural carver in New Orleans or Galveston.

Another significant feature of the house is the design of the balcony and porch railing. The second-floor balcony originally did not extend out to the columns but was cantilevered from the wall and may have had suspension cables or rods to aid in its sup-

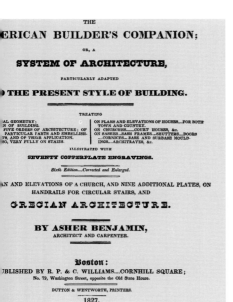

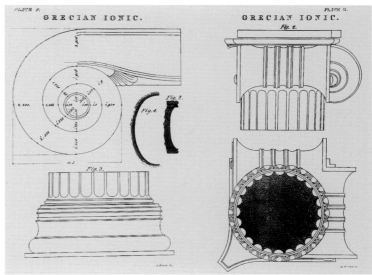

port. At some time, it was extended to the center line of the columns so as to detract somewhat from the visual image of the columns. It is the railing detail, however, that is significant. Here Cook repeats the design which has become, locally at least, his trademark. The "X-and-stick" motif appears on every one of the major houses that he built and on at least one of the smaller houses. This pattern is not original with Cook, but because he used it almost exclusively, it is associated with him. An Abner Cook porch or balcony railing is made up of an arrangement of crossed wood bars, square in section. The origin of the design is probably Roman, and it appears on houses in Georgia, Alabama, and Mississippi, but not, so far as is known, in Tennessee. It is so light and delicate in appearance that it suggests a wrought-iron detail; but, with Cook's skillful joinery, it is stable although very light. It adds a definite elegance to the strong, simple columnar porches of his designs.

In the interior of the Mansion, the most important feature is the sweeping U-shaped stair which terminates the central hall. Here again, the builder's skill is in evidence. The builder's handbooks invariably contain diagrams and instructions for constructing these graceful elements of fine architecture, but only a few builders dared to attempt them. This stairway design is another feature which the Governor's Mansion has in common with the Hermitage. It may, indeed, have been inspired by that example.

The architectural detail of the interior of the Governor's Mansion is extremely simple and yet appropriately large in scale and of good quality in its classical derivation. The six-panel doors

Photographer H.B. Hillyer took one of the earliest Mansion photos in the 1860s. The original unpainted brick is evident.

leading from the hall into the four principal rooms are framed in the Doric style. At the end of the hall, the stair rises in a graceful curve against the semicircular curve of the back wall. The newel and balusters are simple and gracefully turned.

The Mansion's first floor has four rooms opening into the hall; on the right are the two parlors with large sliding doors between them, and on the left are the library and dining room. Each room has a fireplace, except for the dining room which has two. The library, the first room on the left of the hall, has its original mantel. All of the other mantels in the house are replacements.

The windows of the library and front parlor open to the porch and are almost at floor level, allowing easy access between the front rooms and the porch when a lower sash is raised. The second room on the left side of the hall is the dining room which boasts two fireplaces, one at each end of the twenty-three-foot-long room. The interior doors had been "grained" during the Governor E. J. Davis administration, about 1870. In the graining process, the wood was painted in a technique which imitates a fine hardwood such as oak or mahogany. The frames were painted, usually white, as was all of the woodwork.

The second floor repeated the first floor plan with two rooms on each side of the central hall. The central hall, with its door opening onto the balcony, served as a comfortable sitting room in the summer. The architectural treatment of the second floor followed that of the first except that the details may have been even simpler. The location of the semidetached kitchen and service rooms behind the main block of the house were thought to have created an ell, extending to the west along the north line of the house with a porch across the back of the dining room and then along the south wall of the kitchen wing.

The major changes in the Texas executive home took place in 1914 when the old kitchen and service quarters were replaced by a larger, two-story kitchen attached to the main house. A family dining room was added to the first floor. Additional bedrooms and baths were added on the second floor.

Through the years, the exterior of the house had been practically untouched except for periodic painting. With few exceptions such as decorative mantels, the interior walls and woodwork remained as originally built. By 1979, the Mansion was in need of considerable repair and updating in terms of finishes and equipment. Structural reinforcement was essential. The house had to be made sound and safe, and the interior had to be made comfortable and attractive. Pride and interest in the Mansion, along with the support and enthusiasm of Governor and Mrs. William P. Clements, Jr., led the legislature to appropriate funds for repairs. Inspired by Governor and Mrs. Clements, the people of Texas, through the FRIENDS OF THE GOVERNOR'S MANSION, completed the task.

Today, the Texas Governor's Mansion remains remarkably intact, having had relatively few changes in a time span that is fast approaching a century and a half. This restored house in the twentieth century is very much like the structure which Abner Cook built in the nineteenth century. If Governor and Mrs. Pease could return and walk into the house today, they would quickly recognize it as their home of 1856. They would also probably be pleased that the house now reflects the care that the people of Texas have given the home of their governors.

View of the Governor's Mansion from the Capitol, circa 1889. The Davis gazebo is visible on the left.

The Grounds of the Governor's Mansion

AUDRAY BATEMAN RANDLE

Curator, Austin History Center
Austin Public Library

THE SETTING for the Governor's Mansion was of prime importance from its inception. Originally a site to the east of the Capitol, where the Old Land Office now stands, was set aside for the home of the state's chief executive. The location was changed, however, as planning for the actual construction began.

In a report in 1856, the year the Mansion was completed on its new site, the state-appointed Mansion commissioners wrote, "We think it proper to state that if the house had been built on the half block designated by law, there would have been no sufficient room for gardens and shrubbery, and that the house would have had to front so that it could never have been a comfortable and pleasant residence in this climate during warm weather. In changing the location we acted as we would have done if building such a house for ourselves.... We are satisfied all will agree that we have erected the house on the most eligible block in the town where it will, at all times, be a pleasant residence, and a credit to the taste and liberality of the state."

Although provisions for grading and adding topsoil, as well as fencing the lot, were deleted from the original contract, within a short time the legislature made additional appropriations. By 1858, the *Texas Almanac* carried a description of the governor's house. "This is a brick edifice located upon the eminence of the west side of Congress Avenue, near the Capitol. It is two stories, having a portico extending along its whole front, with six Ionic columns and a square roof. It is enclosed by a neat paling with graded ground and is a neat structure."

When Governor Pease moved into the Mansion, construction was not completed. He was without the help and support of his wife, Lucadia, who had gone to Connecticut with their young daughters to visit relatives. As soon as the furniture was arranged, the governor turned his attention to the yard and a garden for the family food supply. In July, his letter to Lucadia reported: "We had a fine shower yesterday afternoon, which was much needed, and it is threatening rain again today. I had the boys all engaged in setting out Bermuda grass; that which I had set out the last rain is looking finely and I hope to have a fine grass plot in the front yard before you return."

After Lucadia and their two little daughters returned to Austin in 1856, she wrote her mother and sisters regularly. She was, at times, homesick for her native state, and to make the Austin surroundings seem more like New England, she planted seeds and cuttings she brought back with her. She later planted seeds that she had ordered by mail or that friends had sent her.

"We are in the midst of gardening," she wrote in February 1857, "and the seeds were very acceptable. Have planted peas, Irish potatoes, and most of the early vegetables. You know we have no very decided summer seasons here, and one day will be windy and cold and the next quite summer like." In a letter a few days later, she wrote that shrubbery and fruit trees had been set out in the garden and yard at the expense of the state.

The gardens and the yard received much attention from the Pease family through the months that they resided in the executive house. In the summer, Lucadia wrote of the great need for rain and reported occasionally on what was blooming in the garden. Since the Pease family had boarded with Thomas William Ward and his wife while the Mansion was under construction, Lucadia especially appreciated the large yard around her new home and all the activities it afforded. "We have just killed six hogs and I am deep in the buslness of lard making and curing hams," she wrote in February 1857. "We shall put up twelve hogs this winter and hope to have enough."

Reports on the grounds and gardens during the following years are scarce. It is known that a stable was completed shortly after Governor Pease left office in December 1857. During the years of the Civil War (1861–1865) and the Reconstruction period in Texas (1865–1873), the state had little money and only the most necessary appropriations for the Mansion were made. It is recorded that during Pendleton Murrah's administration (1863–1865), shingle roofs were put on the outbuildings and some fencing was done.

The Union Army came south within a month after the surrender of Galveston in 1865. The *Austin State Gazette* reported that a portion of the New York Cavalry arrived in Austin, and General Merritt and his staff established headquarters at the Governor's Mansion. There were reports of vandalism during the decade and of a variety of tenants, which left the Mansion in a disreputable condition. No doubt the grounds were left strictly to the care of Mother Nature.

The first gardener, William Davenport, was hired by the wife of Governor E. J. Davis in 1870. While extensive renovation was taking place inside the house, Mr. Davenport began a landscaping project. A thousand loads of topsoil were brought in to enrich and to level the gardens. The backyard, screened from view by a new fence, contained an area for vegetables and more flowers. First Lady Anne Elizabeth (Lizzie) Davis ordered seeds and plants from Maryland, Pennsylvania, and New York. The orders show quantities of petunias, narcissus, hyacinths, tea roses, holly-

hocks, and many other varieties. Herbs and vegetables were ordered for the back area. By the summer of 1871, First Lady Lizzie Davis and Mr. Davenport had completed the landscaping. The front lawn was planted with grass and decorated with wooden benches and cast-iron vases on pedestals. Gravel paths wound through the yard. In the late 1870s, small fountains were added on each side of the front walk. It is believed that Mrs. Davis also added the gazebo.

Around 1890, the Mansion grounds had become overgrown with weeds. This photograph clearly shows the Mansion's dark trim and extended upstairs balcony.

In the nineteenth century, responsibility for making the Mansion a comfortable and attractive residence was left to the governor. The family was free to make changes in the house and surroundings to fit their tastes and needs.

As the Victorian period reached its peak, the brick was painted buff tan, and the trim, including columns and shutters, was painted dark green. The majestic columns in front of the Mansion were covered in vines, and around the house, the shrubbery grew thick and tall. Potted plants adorned the front porch, and Mrs. Davis's cast-iron vases were filled with trailing plants. The wooden rockers on the porch were probably frequently occupied by Austin ladies who came to call on the first lady.

The family of Governor James Stephen Hogg moved into the Mansion in 1891. "For the Hogg children, the years in the

Around 1900, the Austin streets were still unpaved, but the Mansion looked neat and well maintained. The new Carriage House can be seen on the right.

Mansion were a sheer delight," wrote Robert C. Cotner in his biography of the governor. "The commodious block of ground that surrounded the house was divided into smaller plots of fascinating uses: a well-kept front lawn, a croquet lawn, a pool, flower beds, vegetable garden, and a space for fruit trees that included fig, peach, plum, and quince. Next to the stable in the back was a large plot, used both as a running ground and as a playground for the children. Mrs. Hogg took charge of the flower garden, and the governor enthusiastically made the vegetable garden and the fruit trees his provinces. The children hovered around all plantings, growings, and harvestings, helping when they were allowed."

An eight-foot cage in the yard held a menagerie of rabbits and squirrels. Another cage contained cockatoos and other unusual birds. "Jane" was a green and white parrot with a red head, who flew freely about the house and the grounds. The bird waited for the governor to return to the Mansion each day for the noon meal, and as Governor Hogg came up the front walk, Jane would fly out to meet him, crying, "Papa, Papa!"

With each first lady came a few changes in the grounds. Orline Sayers was the first lady at the turn of the century. She greatly simplified the garden areas and removed the fountains. She had

large rose beds planted on the south lawn. Fannie Campbell, wife of Governor Thomas M. Campbell (1907–1911), found the grounds neglected and overgrown. Under her direction, a sidewalk was built around the entire property, the lawn was properly terraced, and the remains of the ancient fence were removed.

The coming of the automobile and improved train service meant that the governors and their families could go home for frequent visits and holidays. The executive house in Austin became only a part-time residence for most of the occupants.

In 1915, after Governor and Mrs. Jim Ferguson moved into the Mansion, First Lady Miriam Ferguson built a greenhouse on the south side of the property. She also had the flower beds and boxes on the gallery planted with brilliantly colored blooms. When she herself was elected governor and returned to the Mansion in 1925 and again in 1933, Mrs. Ferguson continued to enjoy her favorite flowers.

Young Dan Moody was elected governor in 1927. He brought to the Governor's Mansion a bride, Mildred Moody, who immediately won the hearts of the Austin citizens. Like many first ladies, she found time in a busy schedule to improve the house and grounds. She turned the vegetable garden on the north side of the house into a flower garden, which included beds of plants, stone seats, and a trellised arbor hedged with ligustrum. A silvered gazing globe reflected an image of the Mansion. The iron-railed, cement front steps were added during the latter part of the Moody administration.

Snow covered the grounds of the Mansion in 1929. Governor Miriam Ferguson's greenhouse can be seen on the left.

89

Governor Neff and his family admire the plants in the gardens near the greenhouse.

Governor Dan Moody with pet deer on the Mansion grounds. The Carriage House is visible in the background.

Young deer were kept in a large pen on the south lawn during Governor Moody's administration. The animals were often fed through the wire fence by local children and were sometimes photographed by visitors touring the grounds. Years later, Mildred Moody recalled the misfortune of a man who took hold of one of the animals by the horns, and to his embarrassment a horn came off in his hand. Evidently he didn't know it was that time of year when bucks shed their antlers, and the poor man stood there horrified.

A vegetable garden was moved from time to time, but it is believed that one existed into the middle 1930s. The family of Governor Allred was supplied with green beans, radishes, onions,

new potatoes, beets, and lettuce. When one row was used up, the gardener, Mr. Robert Reed, sowed more seeds so that the vegetables were constantly replaced.

The Mansion grounds have been the scene of many large gatherings through the years. When Governor W. Lee O'Daniel took the oath of office in 1939, he invited all the citizens of Texas to his inauguration at the University of Texas Memorial Stadium and to a barbecue on the grounds of the Mansion afterward. The lawn was filled with people on another occasion, the wedding reception of his daughter, Molly.

In the 1940s, azaleas and camellias replaced some of the more standard shrubs, and beds of iris and tulips were planted. Allan Shivers and his family were suddenly the occupants of the Mansion in 1949, due to the death of Governor Beauford Jester. Several years later, Mrs. Shivers said that the chainlink fencing of the Mansion grounds was one of the greatest joys to come her way because it helped corral young Brian during his toddler years.

The garden clubs of Texas enthusiastically endorsed and financially supported Mrs. John Connally's landscaping project in the middle 1960s. Formal rose gardens with terraces, patios, walks,

First Lady Willie Hobby and friends join a group of children on the Mansion steps. The wooden steps and columns were badly in need of a coat of paint.

Dan Moody, Jr. celebrated his birthday with friends in the front yard of the Mansion.

Governor O'Daniel invited Texans to a barbecue on the Mansion lawn.

First Lady Nellie Connally devoted much of her time to the improvement of the Mansion grounds. She raised private funds and involved garden clubs from throughout Texas in a successful effort to totally redesign the grounds and formalize the gardens.

and colonnades were created to give the proper setting for the Greek Revival house. Bricked areas on the west side added the necessary parking space and provided a large area for entertaining. The iron fence that once surrounded the Capitol was removed from storage and incorporated into the brick wall that outlines the two-acre plot. Today, the Mansion grounds remain much the same.

The gardens, often called "Grecian gardens," have been the setting for many social events. In 1968, the marriage of Sharon Connally, daughter of Governor and Mrs. John Connally, was the first to take place in the outdoor setting that has also been described as a "Garden of Eden." The white tents that were used for the reception were put up again in 1972 for the wedding of Governor and Mrs. Dolph Briscoe's daughter, Janey. The young couple exchanged their vows before an altar made of bowers of greenery and surrounded by Victorian bouquets of flowers. The warm December night was lighted by chandeliers filled with a thousand candles.

The traditional Easter egg hunt has been held on the lawn since the Ferguson era. For many years, Mr. and Mrs. Homer Leonard provided hundreds of eggs for the annual Easter egg hunt. (Leonard had been Speaker of the Texas House in 1941.) Children of legislators, friends of the governor, and children from the Austin community have searched for eggs and prizes beneath the spring flowers and near the trunks of the towering trees. In

93

recent years, the Legislative Ladies Club has sponsored this event when the legislature is in session.

Throughout the year and especially in the springtime, organizations from all over the state are entertained on the grounds of the Mansion. Guests stroll about the beautifully landscaped lawn, enjoying the beds of tulips, pansies, and daffodils.

The role of the Governor's Mansion has changed through the years. Originally built to be the home of governors and their families, it is now a historic site to be enjoyed and visited by all Texans. Today, security cameras and a corps of guards carefully monitor the beautifully landscaped grounds that once contributed to the First Family's food supply and stabled the family horses. The Governor's Mansion with its grounds is one of Austin's proudest showplaces. Once a part of the past, it is now restored and a part of the future.

Elisha Marshall Pease

Lucadia Pease

The People Who Lived
in the Mansion

JACK MAGUIRE

University of Texas Institute of Texan Cultures
San Antonio, Texas

For 126 years, calling the house at 1010 Colorado Street in Austin a "mansion" did not make it a home. The house Texas built in 1856 for its governors had eighteen rooms. And the imposing Greek Revival structure built by master builder Abner Cook was one of the capital's most beautiful residences. But while it may have been adequate for the likes of Sam Houston (its third tenant), it was not for a modern head of state.

Governors are expected to host touring dignitaries ranging from U.S. presidents to royalty, plus delegations from all over. If more than one couple spent the night, others had to use rollaway beds or go to a hotel. There was only one guest room. For dinner guests, there was only a single powder room on the first floor. That accommodation was not added until 1941 when Governor Coke Stevenson converted the Green Room into a bedroom for his terminally ill wife and added a half bath.

With large receptions (Governor W. Lee O'Daniel had 20,000 guests at his daughter's Mansion wedding), the restroom problem was acute. Guests had to traipse two long blocks to the Capitol to use the public facilities.

Such events also created havoc in the kitchen. Cooking and serving meals from the tiny kitchen became a juggling act. As late as the tenancy of the John Connallys (1963–1969), it was necessary to scrounge for extra silver and crystal when guests came. The Allan Shivers, residents from 1949 to 1957, left enough silver flatware for twenty-four guests. Needs above that had to be borrowed from Austin friends or rented.

None of these problems was intended by the visionaries who planned the Mansion. In 1854, when Governor Elisha Marshall Pease, State Treasurer James H. Raymond, and State Comptroller James B. Shaw were named by the legislature as special commissioners to provide a home for the chief executive, they had grandiose plans. In one of their reports, they wrote:

> We believe it to be the design of the Legislature, that a residence for the Governors should be built and furnished throughout, so that in future a Governor elect—let him come from what part of our Great State he may—from far, or near, the seat of Government, he would find a building complete in accommodations and furniture, for the occupancy during the term of his office, without the trouble or expense of his looking after, or furnishing any thing requisite to the domestic comfort of himself and family.

Governor Pease, whose family was destined to be the first occupants of the Mansion, had a personal interest in seeing to it that the house would be grand enough to serve the needs of a growing state for all time to come. After all, the decision to spend $14,500 to build a suitable habitation for the governor, plus another $2,500 for furniture, was a magnanimous one. The new state was short of cash. Also, the first four governors after Texas entered the Union in 1845—James P. Henderson, George Tyler Wood, Peter H. Bell, and James Wilson Henderson—had managed to get along without an official residence.

The failure to provide state housing for the chief executive had posed no particular hardship. Frances Henderson, the first First Lady, didn't even bother to come to Austin during the two years her husband was governor. That probably was a great loss to whatever society existed in the primitive village that Austin was in 1846 because Mrs. Henderson was an unusual individual.

She spoke eighteen languages fluently, read in eight others, and was a world traveler who had crossed the Atlantic fifteen times. She was a brilliant mathematician, a talented musician, and a published author. She also was considered to be a Bible scholar,

devoted much of her time to social work and founding churches,
and was an attorney. Probably because San Augustine was then
the cultural center and Austin offered few amenities, she
remained at their East Texas home. Whatever official entertaining that may have been required of the governor was done there,
not at the capital. In Austin, Governor Henderson lived at a
hotel.

The second governor, George T. Wood, seemed perfectly content to have a room and take his meals at Bullock's Hotel. His
wife, Martha, made only one trip to Austin during his term and
that was to attend his inauguration—an event remembered by
historians because the new governor took the oath of office sans
his socks. This was not a sartorial oversight since Governor
Wood continued to go sockless throughout his term. Mrs. Wood
remained at their home in Pointblank, San Jacinto County, taking care of all the business of their plantation and raising five
children. Governor Wood commuted between Austin and his
home whenever possible, riding on his mule, Pantelete.

The third governor to serve without an official residence was
Peter H. Bell. A bachelor who wore his hair shoulder length and
sported a black beard was not much on entertaining and had no
need of a house. Like his predecessors, he lived in an Austin
boardinghouse. He liked the office and is remembered for settling
the boundary dispute that ceded half of what now is New Mexico, plus portions of Kansas, Oklahoma, Colorado, and Wyoming
to the U.S. for ten million dollars. He resigned in 1853 after
being elected to the U.S. Congress.

He was succeeded by James W. Henderson, who had been his
lieutenant governor. Bell's resignation was to give Henderson
the shortest gubernatorial term in Texas history—only twenty-three days. Henderson would not have had time to settle into a
governor's mansion if one had existed because he assumed the
office on November 23, 1853, and left it on December 21.

When E. M. Pease was sworn in as the fifth chief executive to
hold the office after statehood, there still was no official residence. However, this lack did not dissuade the new governor and
his lovely wife, Lucadia, from moving to the capital. At Brazoria,
where Pease had established a successful law practice, they had
built a comfortable home and furnished it with beautiful things
brought from Lucadia's family place in Connecticut. Rather than
move these possessions to Austin, they sold most of them and
arranged to room and board in the home of William (Peg Leg)
Ward. Colonel Ward, a hero of the Revolution, was serving in
Panama as U.S. consul. His wife, Susan, was delighted to have
the new governor and his family as paying guests.

Following his inauguration on December 21, 1853, Governor
Pease settled in for a first term that was destined to be successful. One of his first acts was to steer through the legislature a bill

setting aside two million dollars of the ten million dollars Governor Bell had received in the Compromise of 1850 as a Permanent School Fund. Pease signed the bill on January 31, 1854, and thus is credited with establishing the state's first viable public school system. He also pushed railroad construction, obtained the first appropriations to establish a state university, and established institutions for the hearing-impaired and mentally ill.

It was the building of the new Executive Mansion to which he devoted a great deal of time and personal interest. Since it appeared that he and his family would be the first occupants, he did what any husband contemplating the building of a new home would do: he brought his wife, Lucadia, into the planning. As might be expected, both the governor and his wife had some ideas that were not quite in accord with those of the architect.

One was the proposed location. The legislature had specified that the Mansion be built on the southeast corner of the Capitol grounds where the Old Land Office now stands. There was plenty of room-the original Capitol was much smaller than the present one, and the planners thought that the governor's residence would not only enhance the grounds but would make commuting from home to office more convenient.

Lucadia Pease objected. She wanted it built on a hill fronting Colorado Street between 10th and 11th streets. This would place the Mansion a good four-minute walk from the Capitol but would provide the governors who lived there with an unobstructed view of their workplace. Also, the grounds would be large enough to provide room for the necessary stables and plenty of space for Mrs. Pease, a devoted gardener, to follow her hobby. The commission, headed by the governor, agreed to the relocation, and work began.

Slaves made the brick for the building, and the logs needed for the lumber were hauled by oxen from the pine forests at Bastrop. As work progressed, the two prospective first tenants made further changes.

When it was discovered that the building as planned could not be built with the funds available, the plans for the two wings were dropped. The kitchen, with only a dirt floor, had been designed as separate from the main house. With the revision of the plans, it was built as a semi-detached wing with servants' quarters upstairs. The only detached buildings were the carriage house and a single lean-to bathroom, which would serve both the executive family and the staff.

To furnish the house on the twenty-five hundred dollars voted by the legislature, Governor Pease sent his friend, S. M. Swenson of Austin, to New York. Swenson, a banker and merchant, had excellent taste, and his selections pleased Mrs. Pease. Swenson ran out of money, however, before his task was completed. His frugal buying had been adequate to furnish the downstairs and one bedroom, but the other three bedrooms were bare.

When the contractor missed the January completion deadline by six months, the Mansion Committee deducted $435 from the $14,500 due him. That was the rental the Wards had charged the state to provide room and board for the governor's family while they waited to move into their new home. Finally, on June 14, 1856, the Mansion was officially turned over to the state.

That summer had been particularly hot and humid. It also was a busy one for Pease who was trying to get his new home completed while also dealing with the legislature. Lucadia, uncertain as to their moving date, visited her family's New England home with the children. Thus, there was no formal opening of Texas' first planned Executive Mansion.

Uninvited callers may have provided some humor in Pease's busy life. One day when the doorbell rang, Governor Pease answered it himself, wearing only a shirt and pantaloons. The lady caller inquired if the governor was at home, and he assured her that he was and invited her into the library to wait. Then he went upstairs, put on his coat and vest, and returned to introduce himself as the governor. Later he wrote Lucadia, who was visiting in New England, about the incident.

Austin citizens were curious about the governor's new home. Each evening, there was a parade of buggies up 11th Street as residents drove by and admired the exterior. This inspired Governor Pease to host the Mansion's first social event.

It was a *levee,* a French term for a reception. By whatever name, it was a success. More than five hundred people responded and three hundred stayed for supper. It cost the governor $121,

Governor's Levee.

A LEVEE WILL BE GIVEN AT THE

EXECUTIVE MANSION
ON THE TWENTY-THIRD INST.,

AT EIGHT O'CLOCK, P. M.

☞ THE EXECUTIVE presents his respects to his friends and the public, and will be pleased to meet them on that occasion.

AUSTIN, August 20th, 1856.

Governor Pease's original invitation to the first party at the Mansion.

including $8.30 for broken dishes. By today's standards, that was the bargain of the century because the menu included six turkeys, twenty-four chickens, two pigs, forty loaves of bread, five pounds of butter, cakes, ten pounds of almonds, ten pounds of candy, and brandied preserves and peaches made by Mrs. Pease. As her husband wrote her shortly after: "It was the first public party ever given by the Governor of Texas, and I felt anxious that it should be a creditable one, as it will be the standard by which others to be given by my successors will be measured."

The Peases established elegant entertaining in a capital that had fewer than twenty-five hundred residents, even including members of the legislature when it was in session. During their years in the Mansion, Pease parties included table-rappings (popular at the time), a variety of card games, and dances that were the focus of Austin society.

When Hardin Richard Runnels moved into the Mansion on December 21, 1857, as the sixth governor of Texas, social life at the Mansion slowed somewhat. Runnels, only the second bachelor to hold the office, was not given much to entertaining. Some years before, he had been engaged to an East Texas beauty and had built her a mansion in anticipation of their marriage. The lady changed her mind, however, and Runnels concentrated his interests on politics rather than love.

He was exceptionally successful in that pursuit, beating the popular Sam Houston for the governor's office by almost six thousand votes. This unexpected victory, which followed his broken engagement, put him in the Executive Mansion without a first lady. He solved the problem by inviting his brother, then serving as a state senator, to move into the Mansion with his wife. For the two years he spent in office, his hostess was Martha Caroline Runnels, his sister-in-law.

Runnels tried for reelection in 1859 with Sam Houston as his opponent again. This time, however, the hero of San Jacinto, who twice had been elected president of the Republic of Texas, prevailed. On December 21, the Houstons and their seven children moved into the Mansion.

Surprisingly, their residency there was not a particularly happy one. Austin citizens had not forgotten that it was Houston, as president of the Republic, who had moved the capital away from Austin. What they never knew, or understood, was his reason. He had ordered the move primarily because the new nation had not provided any kind of housing in the new capital for the chief executive.

Houston was deeply in love with his third wife, Margaret Lea. She was only twenty-one and he was forty-seven when they married, and he disliked being separated from her for any length of time. When he was reelected in 1841 for his second term as president of the Republic, his predecessor, Mirabeau B. Lamar,

Sam Houston   Margaret Lea Houston

already had selected the site on the Colorado River as the new capital. Houston did not want to bring Margaret Lea to Austin for reasons other than a lack of suitable living quarters.

Waterloo, as Austin then was known, was a tiny village. Indians still raided its outskirts with regularity, and Houston was concerned for his family's safety. Also, the former general who had led Texas to independence from Mexico felt that there was still danger of a Mexican invasion and that Waterloo would be a target. Another problem was Margaret Lea's health. She had constant bouts with malaria and frequent attacks of asthma.

Houston, probably on the advice of his old friend, Dr. Ashbel Smith, decided that she would be better off remaining in the humid Gulf Coast climate. He went on to Waterloo, but when Congress adjourned on February 5, 1842, he rode his mule back to Houston and Margaret. For several months, he kept the government there, then moved it to Washington-on-the-Brazos. Austin, of course, was well established as the capital when Houston returned as governor in 1859, but the citizens never quite forgave him for his earlier disaffection for the town.

Perhaps the tensions between the town and the chief executive could have been eased some if Margaret Lea had not been pregnant. She did not feel up to the kind of entertaining that Lucadia

Pease had established and that Austin society expected of the Houstons. If she had felt better and had been more willing to host teas and dinners, she likely could have won over the community with the force of her own personality. Those few intimates that she had considered her warm, friendly, and a good conversationalist.

Even if they had tried, however, the Houstons probably could not have overcome the town's feelings about them. Austin was the center of the Secessionist movement, and Houston was pro-Union. Because of his stance, he was no longer the popular idol he had been at San Jacinto and during his presidency of the Republic.

Even the Houston children did not endear the family to the community. Although there were some congratulatory messages when their last son, Temple Lea Houston, was born in the Mansion on August 12, 1860 (the first child of a governor to be born there), the older children were a different story. Six-year-old Andrew Jackson Houston, later to serve briefly in the U.S. Senate by appointment of Governor W. Lee O'Daniel, was especially exuberant. On one occasion, he locked the door of the state senate chamber while that body was in session and hid the key. While the senators fumed, Andrew refused to reveal the hiding place even under threat of a thrashing by his father. It was not until the governor threatened to have him jailed that Andrew turned over the key and allowed the lawmakers to leave.

Despite their active children and their failure to entertain, life in the Mansion might have been happier if Houston had continued the "open door" policy of his predecessors who had issued a standing invitation to all citizens to come and see their governor at any time. Following this practice might have provided Houston another forum from which to expound his pro-Union sentiments. However, in May 1860, he announced that he no longer would see visitors without an advance appointment. It was a policy that was immediately denounced editorially by virtually every newspaper in the state.

Houston had made his anti-Southern stand clear long before he moved his family into the Texas Executive Mansion. As U.S. senator from Texas from 1846 to 1859, Houston's pro-Union sentiments had so infuriated members of the Texas Legislature that they selected his successor two years before his term expired (U.S. senators were not elected by popular vote in those days). His election in 1859 as governor despite his vehement opposition to Secession surprised many Texans, and it certainly did not sway Houston away from his principles.

As governor, he had obeyed the order of the legislature and submitted the question of Secession to a popular vote. He refused, however, to recognize the authority of the Secession Convention that resulted. The man who won Texas its independence from

Mexico at San Jacinto insisted that the act of seceding from the Union made Texas again an independent Republic. As Houston saw the vote to leave the Union, Texans were not necessarily agreeing to join the Confederacy. On that argument, he refused to take the oath of allegiance to the Confederate States of America.

When that happened, the Secession Convention declared the office of governor vacant. There were no formal charges of impeachment and no official action taken by the legislature. Houston, painfully recognizing that he had been deposed although he considered the action illegal, quietly moved his family out of the Mansion to his farm near Huntsville. Edward Clark, his lieutenant governor, assumed the office.

Clark was no stranger to high office. Both his grandfather and father had been governors of Georgia. Already a successful lawyer when he came to Texas and settled in Marshall, he had been both a member of the Annexation Convention and the first state house of representatives. When Governor Henderson, the first to hold the office, vacated it temporarily to fight in the Mexican War, Clark went along as a member of his staff and took part in the battle of Monterrey.

He was elevated to the senate in the Second Legislature, and Governor Pease later chose him as his secretary of state. He had been elected on an independent ticket as Houston's lieutenant governor and thrust into the chief executive's office on March 16, 1861 by the Secession Convention.

This early photograph of the Governor's Mansion was probably taken during the period immediately following the Civil War when no duly elected governor was in residence. The original tan brick is evident, the balcony is unextended, the back porch shows at the rear, and the front steps have no railings.

Clark, his wife, Melissa, and their three children were destined to live in the Executive Mansion less than eight months because he was to lose his try for election to a full term. Their stay saw little social activity because the Civil War had started less than a month after he became governor. The Confederates fired on Fort Sumter, South Carolina, on April 12 and captured it two days later.

Melissa, Clark's second wife and the mother of their three children, was a quiet, plain woman who had little interest in entertaining even if there had been peace instead of war. The few events she hosted during their Mansion stay were limited to small luncheons and dinners for legislators to discuss policy matters with her husband. She was relieved to move out of the Mansion on November 7, 1861, and return to Marshall, leaving problems of state and social obligations to Governor Francis R. Lubbock and his wife, Adele.

Francis Lubbock barely made it to the Executive Mansion, beating Clark by only 124 votes. The arrival of the Lubbocks in Austin delighted the citizenry. Adele Lubbock, a grey-eyed, brown-haired daughter of French Creole parents, loved people. During Lubbock's campaign for the office, she had accompanied him, visiting more than a hundred counties. She charmed the political gatherings with her beauty and her heavily accented English, and she was destined to do the same with the people of Austin.

There had not been an inaugural ball of any consequence since the one given for Governor and Mrs. Pease eight years before, and Austin and Texas were ready for a party. The Lubbocks did not disappoint them. Despite the shortages and other inconveniences of the war, the new governor and his wife managed to entertain more often and more lavishly than any residents of the Mansion since E. M. and Lucadia Pease moved out.

They followed the inaugural ball with the traditional *levee.* That was followed by a succession of parties, dinners, receptions, and other affairs. Governor Lubbock, who had used entertaining to succeed in business, believed that the same technique would work in politics. Almost every evening he and Adele had several members of the house and senate for dinner. These little intimate dinners, usually limited to two or three couples, enabled the governor to get to know the lawmakers and to win their support for his programs.

Apparently two years in the office was enough, however, because Lubbock did not seek reelection. He joined the Confederate Army and became the aide-de-camp to President Jefferson Davis. After the war, he returned to Austin, ran for state treasurer, and served five successive terms in that office.

Whereas the tenure of the Lubbocks in the Executive Mansion had provided an exciting time for Austin society, the time that

Pendleton Murrah, the tenth governor, and his wife spent there
was dreary. When he assumed office on November 5, 1863, the
Civil War was at its height, and local living conditions in the capital were at their worst. There was no inaugural ball. This was no
time for levity. The food served at the small inaugural dinner was
both plain and sparse. The cake was made of cornmeal because
flour had become an unobtainable luxury.

Murrah's wife, Susie, was the youngest first lady at only
twenty-eight. Daughter of a wealthy plantation owner in East
Texas, she had married Murrah when she was only fifteen.
Contemporary reports indicate that the marriage was not a
happy one.

In their book, *First Ladies of Texas,* Mary D. Farrell and Elizabeth Silverthorne tell this poignant story about the Murrahs'
relationship. It seems that a log rolled out of a Mansion fireplace
one winter night and threatened the building. Murrah rushed to
his wife's bedroom and carried her to safety at a neighbor's house.
When he left to check on the fire, Susie burst into tears.

She then related how, on their wedding night, Murrah had
never come to her bed. Through her sobs, she told the neighbors
that when he was carrying her away from the Mansion fire, he
had called her, "My dear!" It was, she said, the first affectionate
words he had spoken to her since their marriage.

Whatever their personal relationship may have been, the Murrahs had few social contacts during their almost two years in the
Mansion. Contemporary accounts indicate that this overt lack of
empathy with the community was not because either of the
Murrahs disliked people. Food was in such short supply that the
little available was hoarded for family use. Times were so bad
that even members of the legislature brought nails and tobacco
to barter for room and board while they were in the capital. Most
camped out on the Capitol grounds, cooking their food over a
campfire.

Since that time, legend has it that the Mansion has been
haunted. Some say that it is the spirit of Sam Houston that stalks
the halls, but most believe that a rejected lover is the authentic
ghost.

Governor Murrah's beautiful niece was a guest, and one of her
male cousins came to visit also. He fell in love with her and
apparently thought she returned the sentiment. However, she
rejected his marriage proposal, and he responded by going into
the north bedroom and shooting himself.

Although the house has had many renovations, strange noises
still can be heard coming from the north bedroom on occasion.
Also doorknobs have been known to turn of their own accord. At
least, these ghostly doings have been reported by former
residents.

Other sources say that if there is a Mansion ghost, it likely is the restless spirit of Governor Murrah who wants to return and finish his term. He is the only chief executive ever to leave the office of his own free will without even bothering to resign or notify his lieutenant governor. In June 1865, he simply locked the governor's office in the Capitol, got on his mule, and rode to Mexico with a coterie of ex-Confederate soldiers. They were fleeing to that country for protection because they feared retaliation against them by Union authorities.

Governor Murrah, his health weakened by tuberculosis and his heart broken by the defeat of the Confederacy, was one who believed in the reality of such retaliation. As governor of an important "enemy" state, he feared he might be sentenced to hang or at least sent to prison. Without so much as a goodbye to Susie, he rode south with the remnants of General Joe Shelby's once-proud army. Murrah reached Mexico safely but died in Monterrey two months after he left Austin.

The unexpected departure of Murrah resulted in Texas having two governors for awhile. Fletcher S. Stockdale, the lieutenant governor, assumed the office and performed the duties for at least a month. He did not move into the Mansion, and most historians do not even list him as ever having been chief executive. However, he deserves at least a footnote in history as "the Governor who wasn't."

The man who succeeded Murrah was not elected and did not bother to take over his duties for a time. He was Andrew Jackson Hamilton, a former attorney general of Texas who also had served in the legislature and as a member of Congress. He was a staunch Unionist, so when Murrah left the office vacant, President Andrew Johnson appointed Hamilton as provisional governor. He was to serve less than fourteen months in the office, but he probably did as much as any leader could to restore civil government, fill vacant offices, and cooperate with the military authorities.

Actually he had held the office previously, although he chose not to govern. President Abraham Lincoln had named him military governor of Texas early in the war, but Hamilton had stayed mostly in New Orleans or Washington and not bothered to return to his state. Thus it was not until July 21, 1865, that the Hamiltons journeyed to Austin, which had been their home, and moved into the Executive Mansion.

By this time, economic conditions had shown some improvement. Hamilton and his wife, Mary Jane, resumed the social life the capital expected of the governor. Food was still in short supply and prices were high, but the Hamiltons managed to resume the traditional *levees* and receptions. It was not easy, however, for a staunch supporter of the Union to entertain in a community where virtually all of the residents had been dedicated to the

Confederate cause. When elections were allowed again in 1866, he did not seek the office, leaving the contest to former Governor Pease and a physician from Collin County, Dr. James W. Throckmorton.

To the surprise of almost everyone in Texas, Throckmorton defeated Pease by a more than four-to-one margin. Winning an election in post–Civil War Texas, however, was not necessarily a clear mandate from the people. Throckmorton knew that he would be under considerable pressure from the U.S. Congress and the military, and he assumed the office with doubts that he would finish the term.

Annie Throckmorton was an intelligent woman, well-read in the classics and in her husband's medical journals. She assumed that his stay as governor would be so brief that she did not bother to move to Austin. Also, the Throckmortons had twelve children—ten of their own and two nieces for whom they were foster parents. Annie felt that the Governor's Mansion simply could not accommodate fourteen people.

Her evaluation of both the available housing in Austin and Texas politics proved to be correct. While she kept the family on the farm, Throckmorton worked hard to rebuild state services and bring order out of chaos. His leadership, however, was not satisfactory either to the radical elements in Congress or the military. On July 30, 1867, General Phil Sheridan, who had an intense dislike for Texas anyway, restored military rule. Nine days later, Throckmorton moved out of the Mansion.

To replace him, Sheridan appointed former Governor Pease as provisional governor. However, the Peases did not live in the executive home. During the ten years Pease had been absent from the office, the couple had purchased a mansion of their own—Woodlawn, a home larger than the governor's residence and built by the same architect, Abner Cook. Woodlawn had been closed during the war, primarily because no servants were available. Lucadia Pease and their children were with her relatives in Connecticut when her husband suddenly had the governorship thrust on him again. Governor Pease had decided to

Mapmaker August Koch hand-drew this map of Austin. Streets are labeled and the 1853 Capitol and the Governor's Mansion are visible at the end of Congress Avenue.

board his family in Austin during this term as governor since the war had taken a toll on both the Mansion and Woodlawn.

Pease arranged for General J.J. Reynolds, the military commander of Texas, and his family to occupy the Mansion instead. Social life, however, was almost nonexistent. Lack of servants and the shortage of such basic foods as sugar and flour made entertaining difficult. Reynolds moved out in April 1869, leaving the Mansion either vacant or occupied only by servants for almost a year.

Pease's second service as chief executive was not a happy one. Always the Unionist, he tried to carry out the policies of Reconstruction. However, this led to clashes with the military, and he resigned in disgust on September 30, 1869.

Once again, Texas had no occupant of the governor's office. The military had failed to appoint a successor to Lieutenant Governor George Washington Jones when he was removed from office along with Governor Throckmorton. For three-and-a-half months, Texas was to be without an executive. The Governor's Mansion continued to deteriorate from a lack of attention.

In the 1869 election, a member of the Radical Republican group in Texas beat former Governor A.J. Hamilton. The winner was a man who had barely escaped hanging by his future constituents only a few years before. In an election most Texans believed was won with illegal ballots, he beat Hamilton by only eight hundred votes.

His name was Edmund J. Davis, perhaps the most feared and certainly the most hated chief executive in the state's history. A virtual dictator, he appointed more than eight thousand to key positions and demanded their unquestioned loyalty. He created a state police force, and when his tyrannical policies caused riots, he used his troops to enforce martial law.

Davis's four years as governor were torn by riots and remembered for the waste, inefficiency, and worse that existed in the government. Although an unpopular governor, Davis did bring about some worthwhile developments. A centralized, free public school system was created; roads and bridges were improved and new ones built; the defenses of the frontiers were strengthened; and the legislature passed a new homestead law.

Because of the long-neglected Mansion, First Lady Lizzie Davis was kept busy bringing about necessary repairs to the Mansion and to the grounds. Most of the people in Austin regarded Davis as having won the office by fraud, and they were not anxious to accept Lizzie as first lady. Most of the entertaining by the Davises consisted of small receptions and dinners for members of the legislature and the thousands he had appointed to public office.

There was one gala occasion at the Mansion, however, and that was the first wedding to be held there. Mary Goodwin Hall, the governor's niece, lived with him and Lizzie, and she married George W. Sampson there in January 1872. It was one of the few happy events during the four years that the Davises were in residence.

Apparently Davis liked both the Mansion and his office, however, because when Richard Coke defeated him by more than two to one in the election of 1873, the governor refused to move out. He declared the election "unconstitutional," an opinion upheld by the supreme court he had appointed. When the legislature met on January 18, 1874, he refused to recognize it. He barricaded himself in the Capitol basement, ordered his secret police to protect him, and wired President U.S. Grant to send Federal troops to help him. When Grant refused, Davis finally moved out of the office and vacated the Mansion.

The assumption of the governorship by Richard Coke was a landmark in many ways because it ended Reconstruction in Texas. Aware that the citizens were weary of war and the shortages and strife that had marked the post-war period, Coke began his term with gaiety. On February 5, 1874, both the senate and house chambers were turned into dance halls, and more than fifteen hundred turned out for what was described as "a grand inaugural ball."

The governor's wife, Mary, was in fragile health and was not up to a heavy civic and social schedule. She was a virtual invalid during their two years in the Mansion. Mary Coke did sponsor the second wedding in Mansion history when a niece of the governor was married there. It was a small event, however, and only a small number of close friends attended as guests.

Coke, who stood six feet, four inches and weighed almost three hundred pounds, was a popular governor and was considered an easy victor for reelection. However, he ran for the U.S. Senate instead and resigned as governor on December 1, 1876.

His successor was Richard Bennett Hubbard, the lieutenant governor, who went on to win election for a full term that same year. When Hubbard and his twenty-seven-year-old wife, Janie, moved into the Mansion just before Christmas in 1876, they brought with them the kind of frequent and formal entertaining that had not existed since E. M. and Lucadia Pease's first years there.

To begin with, the Hubbards demanded some needed changes in the house. The largest individual ever to occupy the office, Hubbard weighed almost four hundred pounds and required an oversized bathtub. This was quickly installed, but the Mansion still did not have running water. The new governor got his water supply later in his term.

Because of the war years and the Reconstruction period that followed, the residence of the governor could hardly be called a "mansion" any longer. It was in a general state of disrepair, the grounds were unkempt, and Janie Hubbard described it as "seedy." Money for rehabilitation and redecoration was not easy to come by, but the Hubbards managed to put the house in shape with a little paint, some new wallpaper, and new curtains.

Once the Mansion had a brighter look, the Hubbards began hosting teas, receptions, and formal dinners. These affairs delighted the people of Austin because the Hubbards often included guests from around the state. The highlight was the wedding of Nettie Houston, the daughter of the hero of the Revolution and the third governor to occupy the Mansion. The wedding, the third to be held in the house, took place on March 1, 1877. Governor Hubbard gave the bride away, and Janie helped prepare the wedding dinner.

Governor Hubbard's bid for renomination at the Democratic convention of 1878 failed when the delegates deadlocked. They finally selected a dark horse, Oran M. Roberts, who had not sought the nomination and was not even present at the convention.

Roberts almost missed being governor because he didn't have fifty cents in his pocket. Although he was a successful Tyler attorney, he didn't have a half dollar when the Democratic Convention wired him and asked him to telegraph his acceptance or rejection of the gubernatorial nomination. He borrowed the money from a friend, sent the telegram, and went on to become the state's seventeenth chief executive.

Roberts, who had been an associate justice of the supreme court and was that body's chief justice at the time he was nominated for governor, was no stranger to politics. He had served a term in the Alabama legislature before moving to Texas in 1841. Both Roberts and his wife, Frances, had grown up on farms, and they brought their love of the land with them to the Governor's Mansion.

Although the Mansion grounds were tiny in comparison with their East Texas farm, Frances planted a vegetable garden soon after they moved in. During their four years there, she kept their table supplied with fresh vegetables in season. Her specialty was raising turnips and greens, but she included tomatoes, radishes, onions, squash, and potatoes on her gardening list. Although it must have surprised the society ladies of Austin, First Lady Frances Roberts insisted on tending the garden personally and often entertained visitors while digging among her plants.

Both the governor and his wife enjoyed people, and they entertained constantly. Except for his inaugural ball and the traditional *levee*, however, these events were plain, in keeping with the country tastes of the governor and his wife. The food served was always plentiful, and many of the cakes, pies, and other goodies were cooked by the first lady.

One of Frances Roberts's contributions to the Mansion was a collection of ash trays. Roberts was known as "the corncob Governor" because he kept one of these "Missouri meerschaums" in his mouth during every waking moment. Even when he stood to be sworn in at his inaugurations, he handed his pipe to a friend so he could place one hand on the Bible and raise his right hand for the oath of office.

Roberts is remembered primarily for his "pay-as-you-go" fiscal policies that not only reduced taxes but left three hundred thousand dollars in the treasury at the end of his term. It was during his administration that a contract was let for the building of a new capitol. Also, the University of Texas opened as he was leaving office.

Roberts's successor, John Ireland, the eighteenth governor, was advised by a newspaper to find living quarters anywhere except the Mansion. Actually Ireland and his wife, Anne Maria, already had moved into the official residence on inauguration day—January 16, 1883. That was three weeks before the Austin *Daily Statesman* published an editorial urging them not to do so.

"The dampness of the walls, the exhalations from vapory and various cellars, the leaky roof and other notable faults make it unfit for human beings to dwell in," the editor wrote. He went on to say that disease "had taken hold of every family occupying it," and that the Hubbard's children became infected with "miasmic poison."

This aerial view of the Mansion was taken in the late 1880s from the roof of the new granite Capitol under construction. The Mansion grounds are covered with trees, and the shutters and cornice are painted dark green.

It was true that two of the Hubbard sons had died three years after the governor's term ended, but their deaths could not be reasonably blamed on germs picked up in the Mansion. At any rate, the Irelands ignored the warnings, made some minor renovations to the house, and continued to live there.

Legend has it that Ireland enjoyed his inaugural ball so much that he danced with Anne Maria twenty-two times. If so, this was a unique event in their lives because Mrs. Ireland was deeply religious and regarded dancing as sinful. She cared little for parties of any kind and limited her activities at the Mansion primarily to official entertaining. However, she did host a reception for their daughter, Rosalie, who became the fourth Mansion bride when she married E. S. Hurt on January 1, 1887.

On January 18, 1887, Lawrence Sullivan (Little Sul) Ross became the nineteenth governor of Texas, and a large crowd turned out for the inaugural ball. The dance was at Austin's new Driskill Hotel, the first of many such affairs to be held there. It seemed that everyone wanted to honor the ex-Indian fighter, Civil War general, and one-time sheriff of McLennan County.

Elizabeth Ross, Lizzie to her husband and friends, was as large as her husband was diminutive. For the inaugural ball, she was a dazzling figure in a heavy black silk dress with a train trimmed with various ornaments. She was still there at daylight greeting old friends, making new ones, and presiding at the banquet tables. The next day, she moved the six Ross children into the Mansion and settled in for four happy years.

Once again the old house was filled with the noise and laughter of children, and both the governor and Lizzie encouraged them to entertain their friends there. The family also maintained an almost continuous open house for Austin citizens, visitors from around the state, and political leaders.

Texas loved Lawrence Sullivan Ross. He is the only governor to have a college named in his honor—Sul Ross State University at Alpine. At Texas A&M University, where he served as president after leaving public office, the school's crack drill team is called the Ross Volunteers. Ross probably could have had a third term if he had asked for it, but his principal interest was higher education. He was eager to assume the Aggie presidency.

In 1894, Governor Hogg posed with his wife Sallie and their four children, (left to right) Ima, Will, Tom, and Michael. This young family brought happy times and gracious entertaining to the house.

The Mansion was in quite a state of disrepair when James Stephen Hogg became the twentieth governor and moved his family into the executive home.

Hogg, the first native son to be elected governor, contributed some other "firsts" to the office. He was the first justice of the peace ever to be elevated to the state's highest office. He also was the first chief executive ever to veto a legislative appropriation intended to lessen the burdens of his office.

In 1893, he was running the governor's office with one secretary, a typist, and a porter. He asked the legislature for an additional fifteen hundred dollars so he could hire a file clerk, and the request was granted. However, when Hogg discovered that the state treasury was in the red, he vetoed the appropriation. "I can, and will, add one or two more hours of service a day to the other employees of the department and do some extra work myself," he told the lawmakers in his veto message.

Hogg also was the first governor to deliver an address via a recording. In the fall of 1905, he was invited to speak to the Legislative Day banquet at the State Fair of Texas in Dallas. Illness prevented his attending. Not wanting to disappoint the audience, he recorded his speech on an Edison phonograph record, and it was played at the meeting.

During their residence from 1891 to 1895, there were no guards, and the public was always welcome. Neighbors often dropped in to join Sallie Hogg for a cup of coffee or to borrow a cup of sugar. It was an era of friendliness and neighborliness that the capital had rarely seen before.

The Hoggs were delighted when his attorney general, Charles A. Culberson, and Sallie Culberson succeeded them as the twenty-first residents of the Mansion. Whereas the Mansion had been a lively place, filled with children, guests, and animals during the Hoggs' residence, it changed drastically with the new tenants.

Sallie Culberson, like several of her predecessors as first lady, was not in good health. While her husband's passion was politics—altogether he served thirty-two years in elected offices and was prominently mentioned as a possible candidate for president—his wife cared little for the political life. Until he became governor, she had a policy of never returning calls and almost never accepted invitations.

Once in the Governor's Mansion, however, Sallie Culberson seemed to relish her new role. Although considered an invalid, she hosted some of the more memorable luncheons, dinners, and parties in history. The legislature, aware of her physical condition, had thoughtfully added a housekeeper to the Mansion staff. She didn't entertain often, but when she did, she insisted that the food and decorations be as close to perfection as possible.

When the Culbersons moved into the Mansion in 1894, they brought their own beautiful rugs, paintings, and many luxurious accessories. However, it concerned Sallie that furniture was moved in and out of the house with each new tenant, and she was fearful that some of the things that belonged in the Mansion permanently might somehow disappear. One of her contributions was to make sure that this didn't happen to the bed that Sam Houston had used. She ordered a silver plate added to the footboard reading:

> This bedstead was used in the
> Executive Mansion
> by
> Governor Sam Houston
> and this tablet placed thereon
> by Mrs. Charles A. Culberson
> to identify and preserve it for
> future generations.
> January 16, 1899.

Despite her fragile health, Sallie Culberson regarded their years in the Mansion as some of the happiest of her life. Her popular husband might have had a third term as governor (unheard of at the time) had he not decided to run for the U.S. Senate instead. He was elected senator, and Joseph D. Sayers became the twenty-second governor of Texas.

Sayers was an old hand at politics. In 1872, he had been elected to the Texas Senate and, in 1878, had served a term as lieutenant governor during the administration of Oran Roberts. In 1885, he was elected to Congress and was serving there when prominent Democrats urged him to run for the state's highest office. In the election of 1898, he won over a trio of opponents by a majority of almost three to one.

If, as some newspapers said, "Sayers was the perfect Governor for the times," his wife, Orline, deserved the same accolade as first lady. Lena, as she was affectionately known, believed the Executive Mansion should be the focus of social life, not only in Austin but in Texas, and that the governor and his wife should set the example for gracious entertaining.

Lena was blessed with exquisite taste, not only in the social amenities but in dress. When she appeared at the inaugural ball on January 17, 1899, wearing a gown of white Battenburg lace adorned with a pearl necklace, society editors described her as "elegant." Leading the grand march with Governor Sayers, a handsome man with snow-white hair and a steel-grey mustache, the couple drew "ohs" and "ahs" from those who had come to get a glance of the new residents of the Mansion.

That great house on a hill west of the Capitol got Lena's attention as soon as the inaugural festivities ended. The Mansion,

The parlors were decorated for a Mansion reception for President William McKinley when he visited Austin during the Sayers Administration.

During the Sayers administration (1899–1903) the Entry Hall was meticulously decorated in the tastes of the time. An ornate coal-burning stove added warmth to the notoriously drafty house and was vented through the outside wall. The stairway spindles and woodwork were dark.

First Lady Lena Sayers posed for this picture on the front lawn about 1899. Mrs. Sayers committed much of her time to improving the Mansion and its grounds during her four-year occupancy.

then into its thirty-fourth year of housing governors and their families, once again was in need of refurbishing. As in the past, the legislature was penurious in providing the funds, but Lena had a knack of making one dollar do the work of two. She managed to get the place repainted, the old stable replaced with the carriage house still in place today, and a rose garden installed on the south lawn.

Inside, she concentrated on making the house look more like a home by retouching the historical paintings herself and installing them in more suitable frames. Since the Sayers expected to entertain often and lavishly, she designated a state bedroom for use of important guests. In the room were placed the Sam Houston bed and other historic furnishings.

Lena's decision to provide suitable overnight quarters for dignitaries proved to be a wise one. During the four years the Sayers spent in the Mansion, their guests included President and Mrs. Theodore Roosevelt, President and Mrs. William McKinley, and notables in and out of government from throughout the country. Almost invariably each prominent guest was honored at a dinner, luncheon, or reception to which prominent Texans were always invited.

One frequent Mansion guest was Elisabet Ney, the famed sculptress who left her native Germany to establish a home and studio in Austin. Before the Sayers administration began, Miss Ney had made plaster casts of Sam Houston and Stephen F. Austin. Despite efforts to find the funds needed to complete the works in marble, the plaster figures had lain for years in the Ney studio. At the behest of Lena, the governor got a bill through the legislature appropriating the money needed to finish the statues. They stand today in the Capitol.

Whereas Joseph and Lena Sayers found their four years in the Mansion rewarding and happy ones, their successors did not. Samuel Willis Tucker Lanham, the twenty-third governor, found his position an almost overwhelming task that was tiresome and disappointing. His wife, Sarah, unlike her active predecessor as first lady, had little interest in entertaining and was something of a social recluse.

This may have been partially because of age. At sixty, Lanham was the oldest man ever elected to the office, and Sarah Lanham was sixty-one. Also, he had served several terms in Congress and found public service at that level rewarding and interesting. By the time he became governor, however, his health had begun to fail. The old orator who had held his colleagues in the house spellbound with his speeches was tired. "I made a great mistake when I became Governor of Texas," he once wrote. "Office-seekers, pardon-seekers and concession-seekers overwhelmed me."

The Lanhams began their residence in the Mansion under unfortunate circumstances. On January 20, 1903, in the excitement of the occasion, the Inaugural Committee forgot to make arrangements to get the new First Family to the oath-taking ceremonies. When no escort came for them, the Lanhams had to walk alone from the Driskill Hotel to the Capitol.

One of the few large social events in which the Lanhams were involved was the inaugural ball for their successors, Thomas M. Campbell and his wife, Fannie. Sarah Lanham and Governor Campbell, as is the custom, led the grand march, January 15, 1907. Sarah was dressed rather simply while the new first lady wore a white satin gown with a long train. The gown was decorated with brocaded roses, accented by pearls.

The inaugural ball, held in an elegantly decorated house of representatives, was the portent of things to come. Fannie Campbell, whose husband had been general manager of the International & Great Northern Railroad, had been a social leader in their hometown, Palestine. Like Lena Sayers, she believed that the obligation of the governor and his wife to the electorate included gala entertaining.

Electric lights had replaced the gas lamps in the Mansion by 1908. Monies that the legislature appropriated for Mansion refurbishing were used to spruce up the exterior and not for added conveniences for the tenants. Both the Campbells believed that the taxpayers' money should be used to benefit all Texans, not just those who were fortunate enough to live in the Executive Mansion. At her insistence, the small appropriations available were used to lay sidewalks around the building, to terrace and landscape the gardens, and to add improvements that any visitor or passerby might see and enjoy.

During their four years in the Mansion, the Campbells entertained often and sometimes lavishly. Fannie particularly liked musicales, but they also hosted luncheons, dinners, and receptions. Governor Campbell shared her enthusiasm for entertaining and tried to find time in his busy work schedule to attend. He often would drop in unexpectedly on Fannie's afternoon teas and musicales if only long enough to greet the guests.

The Campbells had a close relationship in everything they did, and he often said that he had never made a decision without talking it over with Fannie first. Some of the reform legislation for which his administration is remembered—prison reform, the state's first pure food laws, and others—are sometimes credited to Fannie's influence on her husband.

By the time the Campbells vacated the Mansion in 1911, the building was into its fifty-fifth year of service without ever having major structural renovation. Almost every occupant had tried to make some improvements, but there were never enough funds available to do very much during a single administration. This changed, however, with the arrival of Oscar Branch Colquitt, the twenty-fifth governor, and his wife, Alice. During his first

MANSION

term, he convinced the legislature that it was time to spend a little more money than usual in order to put the old house back into first-class condition.

Since the Campbells already had improved the exterior, the Colquitts used the appropriation to do the same for the interior. Alice Colquitt, realizing the constant need of the occupants to entertain, began by modernizing the kitchen. This work was done without disturbing the preparation of meals or the serving of receptions. Mrs. Colquitt simply erected a tent near the rear entrance and temporarily installed the kitchen there while the new equipment was being added inside.

The kitchen was only the beginning. The tan brick exterior was painted white, as was the interior woodwork. Since the house always had been short of bedrooms, two more plus bathrooms, were added on the second floor. The fireplaces remained, but gas radiators were installed for the first time. A family dining room was added downstairs, and the walls throughout were repapered or refinished. Even Sam Houston's bed was given a canopy of pink brocade.

Governor and Mrs. Thomas M. Campbell (1907–1911) posed with their son and three daughters on the Mansion steps. The new Carriage House can be seen to the right. Curbing, new steps, and a lack of fencing have changed the Mansion entrance.

Governor and Mrs. Oscar Colquitt pose on the steps of the newly renovated and expanded Mansion.

This 1912 photograph shows the original house with the smaller kitchen wing and L-shaped back porch. By 1914, this section of the house had been removed, and the new addition that exists today replaced it.

Despite the Mansion's new look, the social life there during the residence of the Colquitts was not memorable. The Colquitts hosted all of the necessary events—the traditional New Year's *levee,* state dinners for visiting dignitaries, and occasional receptions—but they preferred quiet evenings with friends to a constant round of parties.

The Colquitts brought an exciting innovation to the Mansion in that he was the first governor to own and drive an automobile. Like their predecessors, the Colquitts had arrived at the Mansion with a handsome carriage and a pair of fine horses. However, the horses and carriage were rarely used once the car was acquired. It was kept in a downtown Austin garage and brought over several times each week so the family could take driving lessons.

Their successors in the Mansion, Governor James E. Ferguson and his wife, Miriam, arrived in Austin to take the oath of office aboard a private railway car, courtesy of a Santa Fe Railroad official in their hometown of Temple. However, the Fergusons owned a Packard Twin Six auto, and it was to play a special role in their lives.

Austinites learned early on about the car, but it failed to impress them. Having missed the diverting social life of the Mansion during the four years the Colquitts spent there, they predicted that it would be even less exciting when the Fergusons moved in. After all, both the new twenty-sixth governor and his wife had grown up on farms. There was even a legend that Mrs. Ferguson had never been outside of Bell County, her birthplace, and that Temple was the largest town she had ever seen. Their arrival did not impress Austin society.

The capital city was in for a surprise. One of Mrs. Ferguson's first acts was to hire a social secretary. Although she paid the salary of this staff member out of her own pocket, she was roundly criticized by both her husband's opponents and the newspapers for "waste." Most people had never heard the term "social secretary" and had no idea what the job entailed. However, Mrs. Ferguson was well aware of the entertainment responsibilities of a first lady, and she realized early on that she needed help to carry them out.

The fact was that Mrs. Ferguson, like several of her predecessors, cared very little for an active social life. As the wife of a politician, however, she realized the importance of the governor having people in his home. She started off by inviting the entire Thirty-sixth Legislature to the Mansion for a reception on March 2—Texas Independence Day. At Easter, she borrowed a tradition from the White House in Washington and staged an egg roll on the Mansion grounds—an event she hoped other first ladies might continue. She also established two Tuesdays each month as her "at home" days when visitors were welcome to call.

Governor Miriam Ferguson posed with friend Will Rogers and her family and other friends on the front steps in 1926. Ex-Governor James Ferguson is third from the right. The child between Will Rogers and Ma Ferguson is her grandson.

Miriam and Jim Ferguson's daughter, Dorrace, stood with the family pets in the Entry Hall during Ma Ferguson's first administration (1925–1927).

There were, of course, the inevitable state dinners and receptions to honor this group and that. Also, there were many parties for the two Ferguson daughters, Dorrace and Ouida. Planning these constant events, sending out invitations, arranging menus and refreshments, and seeing to the necessary decorations kept both Mrs. Ferguson and the social secretary busy.

First Lady Miriam Ferguson also found time to refurbish the Mansion. The legislature gave her the funds to build a greenhouse so that the Mansion could grow its own flowers for decorating and entertaining. The Mansion roof was repaired, and a garden retaining wall was built. The upstairs porch was also screened in to make a sleeping porch for Governor Ferguson.

Although a successful Temple banker, Ferguson always referred to himself as "Farmer Jim," and the rural folks (who constituted the majority of voters then) loved it. After electing him in 1914, they reelected him in 1916. And they liked what he did. Among other things, Governor Ferguson created the state's first highway department and started the licensing of motor vehicles. He also began the collection of taxes on gasoline, got construction started on the first state office building outside the Capitol grounds, and created the state's first system of senior colleges.

Because he was a strong believer in education, he also located teachers' colleges in every section of the state. He was the first governor to stabilize school terms at nine months, to pass a compulsory attendance law, and to provide free textbooks for students in the elementary grades.

In his second term, however, storm clouds gathered over his administration. Despite his support of education, he elected to wage an all-out war against the University of Texas. He charged university officials with graft, padding payrolls, and the misuse of state funds. When the board of regents refused his order to fire five faculty members, he vetoed the entire appropriation for the school. These acts and others eventually led members of the legislature, many of whom were University of Texas alumni, to file impeachment charges against him.

On August 30, 1917, the formal impeachment trial began in the senate after the house of representatives had voted twenty-one charges against the governor. On September 20, the senate not only found him guilty but prohibited him from ever again holding an office of honor, trust, and profit in Texas. Lieutenant Governor William P. Hobby, Sr. of Houston assumed the office. Farmer Jim, calling the legislature a "kangaroo court," announced that he was going back to "my stock and my hogs."

This was when the Packard Twin Six assumed its role in history. It was in the Packard that the Fergusons, the shadow of impeachment upon them, drove away from the Executive Mansion that fall day in 1917. Mrs. Ferguson was driving. As they left the grounds, she tried to cheer her husband by telling him that one day the same car would bring them back to the Mansion again.

The Fergusons returned to their Victorian house in Temple. Farmer Jim, despite the prohibition against his ever holding office again, made an unsuccessful effort to win reelection as governor. He also had started a weekly newspaper, the *Ferguson Forum,* and used it to lambast his enemies and carry on his fight for vindication. After two years, the Packard, its tires worn thin and its engine in need of repair, was stored in a Temple garage.

The car remained in the garage in 1920 when Ferguson made a try for the White House as the candidate of the American (Know Nothing) Party and lost. It stayed in storage in 1922 while he campaigned for the U.S. Senate and lost again. Then, in 1924, Texas voters elected Mrs. Ferguson as their governor—the first woman in the U.S. ever elected to the office.

Mindful of her prediction of eight years before, Mrs. Ferguson had the Packard removed from storage. She equipped it with a new battery and new tires and had it polished until it shone like new. Mechanics went over the motor, putting it in first-class running order. On January 19, 1925, with the governor-elect at the wheel and her husband at her side, she drove the Packard from Temple to the Executive Mansion in Austin. The Fergusons had returned to power in Texas politics.

She was to lose her bid for a second term in 1926, and she was also defeated in 1930 when she tried for the office again. The Fergusons were persistent, however, and when she ran again in 1932, she was elected for another two years. She sought still another term eight years later, but by 1940, the electorate had changed. The old slogan of "two Governors for the price of one" did not work, and the Fergusons were retired forever from the political scene.

Between the interrupted reigns of the Fergusons, various others held the office of governor and occupied the Mansion. Lieutenant Governor William P. Hobby, Sr., who succeeded to the office in 1917 when Jim Ferguson was impeached, served out that unexpired term and was reelected for another.

When Hobby and his wife, Willie, moved into the Mansion as its new tenants, war again was the primary concern of the people. This time, it was not strife between the North and the South like that which had split the nation less than six decades before. This was a world war, and a united nation geared for battle against a common foreign aggressor. The conflict again restricted social life at the Mansion, and "victory" gardens and volunteer work replaced entertaining as the principal interests of the first lady.

Occasional dinners and luncheons were hosted by the Hobbys if their purpose was not altogether social. And when Willie's personal maid, Savannah Jackson, fell in love with a Capitol porter and decided to marry him, Governor and Mrs. Hobby invited them to hold the ceremony in the Mansion. The surroundings proved especially impressive to the minister who was presiding, and he concluded the wedding with these words: "Now, in the presence of Almighty God—and the Governor of Texas—I pronounce you man and wife."

For their successors as Mansion residents, the Hobbys left an important legacy—steam heat. The old house, which had depended on fireplaces and the gas radiators that the Colquitts had installed to keep its tenants warm, had never had the luxury of a central heating system. When critics warned that such an extravagance could cost Hobby reelection, Willie replied: "I'd rather be warm for two years than freeze for four."

After three-and-a-half years in the comfortably warm Mansion, the Hobbys were succeeded by the twenty-eighth governor, Pat M. Neff, and his wife, Myrtle. A Baptist lay leader, Governor Neff did not approve of dancing, so neither of his inaugurations (on January 18, 1921 and January 16, 1923) was followed by the traditional ball. There were receptions, but punch was the strongest drink served.

The new governor did not drink alcohol, coffee, or tea, so refreshments at Mansion functions were limited to fruit drinks. Myrtle Neff continued the "at home" Tuesdays her predecessors had followed, and both she and the governor hosted the functions they felt were required of the office. However, neither cared for the social life, and they remained aloof from it as much as possible.

On January 20, 1925, when the Fergusons moved back into the Mansion after her election as governor, Neff introduced her at the inaugural festivities. In his welcome, he announced that he was leaving a Bible on his desk with a passage from the Psalms marked for her. It read: "Thy word is a lamp unto my feet, and a light unto my path."

Thus began a tradition that Mrs. Ferguson continued. When thirty-three-year-old Dan Moody defeated her in her bid for reelection in a campaign marked by bitter denunciations on both sides, the passage she marked for him was the Golden Rule. However, she did not continue another tradition—that of leaving a hot lunch at the Mansion for the new occupants. "Dan, the Man," as his campaign posters proclaimed, and his beautiful young wife, Mildred, had to provide their own food after the inauguration ceremonies.

Apparently the Fergusons's failure to observe this bit of gubernatorial etiquette did not bother the Moodys. Both were exuberant over winning the office in what the press had dubbed the "honeymoon campaign." The couple had been married the previous April, only days before Moody announced for the office,

First Lady Willie Hobby in the Small Parlor.

Hobby Administration—1917–1921

William Pettus Hobby first came to the Governor's Mansion as a result of the Ferguson impeachment. Renewed patriotism accompanied World War I and was reflected in the Mansion by the American flag in the staircase. By this period (1917–1921), the walls were papered to cover the deterioration in the 1856 plaster. The floors were carpeted, except in the Conservatory. The trim paint is a light color throughout the house, and the stairway spindles are painted. The formal cove molding and mantels are in place in the parlors. A wainscoting is evident in the Library, as are today's brass chandelier and the original mantel. Matching doors that flank the Library fireplace lead into the State Dining Room. Musical entertainment could be provided on the piano seen in the main entry.

Governor William
Pettus Hobby and
First Lady Willie
Cooper Hobby on the
front porch.

The Parlors

The Library

The Conservatory

The Entry Hall

The State Dining Room

The Southeast Bedroom

The Upstairs Hall

The Southwest Bedroom

and his bride had traveled with him as he toured the state meeting voters. Delighted to finally be a Mansion resident, Mildred began the job of turning the place into a suitable home for the youngest couple ever to live there.

The Fortieth Legislature appropriated funds for these repairs and some furnishings and also increased the amount set aside for the Mansion maintenance. First Lady Mildred Moody helped in the selection of wallpaper for the house, enlisting a decorator for the first time in the Mansion's history. A French Zuber, scenic wallpaper was chosen for the dining room. Electrical wiring was also replaced, and iron rails and stone steps were added to the front entry. When state funds ran short, Mildred Moody used her own family money to complete the renovation.

The Moody's customary New Year's Eve reception was canceled in 1929 because the first lady was expecting a baby. Dan Moody, Jr. was born January 6, 1929. The Mansion once more had a child in the house.

Mildred Moody left a legacy, the idea of a Board of Mansion Supervisors. She realized that the historic old house needed careful thought in maintaining and preserving it for all times. The next governor, Ross Sterling, appointed the board and named her as chairman.

By 1930, as Moody's term neared its end, economic depression was abroad in the land. He was not a candidate for a third term, and voters turned to a successful oil tycoon as their thirty-first governor. He was Ross Sterling of Houston, founder of the Humble Oil and Refining Company (now Exxon), newspaper

Governor and Mrs. Pat Neff pose with the family on the Mansion steps. The Gothic screen door served a practical as well as a decorative purpose for many years.

This cartoon ran in Collier's, The National Weekly, April 17, 1926.

Taken in the late
1920s, this photograph
shows the Ferguson
screened-in upstairs
porch, tall cedar trees
surrounding the front
steps, fountains on
either side, and Mrs.
Ferguson's greenhouse.

Governor Dan Moody
and wife Mildred
moved into the
Mansion in 1927
as newlyweds.

publisher, and investor. Sterling never wanted to hold public office and always said that the governorship was thrust on him.

When the Sterlings moved into the Mansion on January 21, 1931, they realized that the economy was in such bad shape that entertaining would be kept at a minimum. There was an inaugural ball and reception, but decorations were simple and so were the refreshments.

Maud Sterling did not miss the social events. Her principal hobby was fishing, not parties, and she frequently slipped away from the Mansion to drop a hook in a favorite lake or in the Gulf. An unpretentious woman, she enjoyed cooking (the governor almost always came home for lunch), and she preferred to answer the Mansion doorbell in person.

Because the Sterlings were wealthy when he was elected governor, entertaining even in the midst of a depression would have posed no financial problem for them. However, such expense did—and sometimes still does—pinch the purse of many who have been Mansion residents.

That is because when the governor entertains privately, he has to pay for the food and liquor. The costs of printing and mailing the invitations are also his personal expense. The legislature makes annual appropriations for the upkeep of the Mansion and the Mansion staff. The governor is responsible for all other expenses.

Holding the office had been personally costly for Sterling, and he had seen most of his fortune erode while he was attending the state's business. Despite all this, he decided to seek reelection. Although he had beaten Mrs. Ferguson in 1930 when she had tried for the office a second time, he lost to her in 1932. On

Below left: Ross Sterling taking the oath of office on the Capitol steps, inauguration day January 20, 1931.

Below right: Inaugural procession January 20, 1931. Included in the photo from left to right are Governor Dan Moody, Governor Ross Sterling, Mrs. Maud Sterling, and Mrs. Mildred Moody.

Governor and Mrs. James V. Allred posed with their two sons and "Santa" in the Mansion Library for a family Christmas card during Allred's first administration, 1935–1937.

The Mansion grounds have been used for civic and charitable events throughout their history. This photograph shows Governor Allred with a group of scouts.

State Dining Room

Allred Administration—1935–1939

In 1937, First Lady Joe Betsy Allred and the Board of Mansion Supervisors asked Marcelle Lively-Hamer to produce a brochure on the then present-day Governor's Mansion. In this publication, the Mansion was illustrated only with photographs of the facade and the entry.

The brochure describes the Entry Hall as having green carpet, white woodwork, and a reproduction wallpaper with a "soft green ground." The French Legation loveseats that are now in the Sam Houston Bedroom were in the Entry Hall with the Mansion portraits of Stephen F. Austin and Sam Houston above them.

The parlor walls were covered with a gold and white wallpaper, gold moire draperies framed the windows, and the cornice was described as "gilt." The parlors were carpeted with a "copy of an old Aubusson pattern, with pale pink and yellow roses on a

132

Conservatory   South Entry Door

Library

Original porte cochere

grey ground." The fireplaces had pink tiles and white mantels. A few pieces of First Lady Lena Sayers' French furniture remained in these rooms, and the Mansion Collection grand piano stood in the Large Parlor.

The Library had a "lived-in look" with oak furniture, a toile pattern wallpaper, and dark green carpet and draperies.

Matching doors led to the dining room, its walls still covered with Mrs. Moody's scenic wallpaper. The Hobby radiators provided heat throughout the house. The State Dining Room had green carpet and red damask draperies.

The Family Dining Room was described as "cheerful," with green walls and white woodwork. The doors had a red mahogany finish. A red hook rug, informal curtains, and a ceiling fan set a more casual mood in this room. The furniture was "antiqued green."

January 17, 1933, the Fergusons moved back into the Mansion for their third stay.

On this occasion, the Sterlings broke two traditions that outgoing governors had followed. Not ony did Maud Sterling refuse to leave a hot lunch for the Fergusons, but she and her husband left town and did not attend the inauguration of his successor. The absence of the Sterlings, however, did nothing to dampen the welcome the capital gave the Fergusons. Inaugural balls were held at the Driskill, Stephen F. Austin Hotel, and Gregory Gymnasium on the University of Texas campus.

This time around, Governor Ferguson seemed less interested in the affairs of state than she had during her previous term. Keeping her promise of "two Governors for the price of one," she turned as many duties as she could over to Farmer Jim and spent as much time as she could at the Mansion. She much preferred running a house to running a state.

Mrs. Ferguson did not try for reelection, and James V. Allred became the thirty-third governor on January 15, 1935. Although they had not been political opponents and there was no visible enmity between the two, the outgoing governor again failed to leave the traditional lunch for her successor. Allred and his wife, Joe Betsy, had to follow his inauguration with lunch in an Austin hotel coffee shop.

The Allreds arrived at the Mansion with two lively youngsters, James, Jr. and David. A third son, Sam Houston Allred, was to be born there in the bed made famous by the hero of San Jacinto. From the beginning, the family fell in love with the Mansion, and Joe Betsy tried to make it as homelike as possible. She searched all over Austin for original furnishings that might have been stored by former residents and found several pieces that she had restored and placed in the Mansion.

Like all youngsters, the Allred children were active and provided many stories for the newspapers. One told how young Jimmie discovered a box of candy that one of the Mansion guards had bought for his girlfriend. The youngster ate the candy and then carefully replaced it with pieces of mud.

The antics of the Allred children made tame reading, however, compared with the family of the next governor, Wilbert Lee O'Daniel. In the spring of 1938, O'Daniel, a Fort Worth flour salesman and emcee of a popular hillbilly music show featuring the "Light Crust Doughboys," read a letter from a listener suggesting he run for governor. O'Daniel read the letter over the air, and 54,542 listeners deluged him with messages seconding the idea. He entered the race, won easily without a runoff, and became the thirty-fourth governor.

O'Daniel's own vote was not among those cast for his election, because he was not eligible to go to the polls. Texas had a poll tax in those days, and the candidate had not bothered to pay his. He

Governor W. Lee O'Daniel broadcast to Texans every Sunday morning from the Governor's Mansion. Shown in this photograph are the Governor, Pat Adelman, an Austin radio host, and Mrs. O'Daniel in the background.

First Lady Merle O'Daniel in the State Dining Room. Mildred Moody's Zuber "Scenic America" wallpaper covers the walls.

*Governor and Mrs. Stevenson on
his inauguration day in 1941.*

did not vote for himself when he ran for reelection in 1940 either, but his ballot was not needed. He received 1,019,338 of the 1,079,538 votes cast—the first candidate for the office ever to receive more than a million votes.

He also became the only chief executive not to take the oath of office at the Capitol. He was inaugurated for his first term in Memorial Stadium at the University of Texas. An estimated fifty thousand watched the five-hour ceremony on January 17, 1939. His wife, Merle, and their three grown children, Pat, Mike, and Molly, were on hand, plus assorted relatives, friends, and a multitude from all over Texas. The ceremonies included a pageant, "The American Way of Life," presented by two hundred young people; music by forty college and high school bands; and a sing-along led by dozens of choirs. The celebration concluded with three balls, dancing in the streets, and the biggest fireworks display ever seen in Austin.

For his second inauguration in 1941, he invited all Texans to come to the Mansion for lunch. An estimated nineteen thousand did. Volunteers from thirteen state agencies served 19,000 pounds of barbecue (including a buffalo the governor had shot himself), 1,000 pounds of potato salad, 1,300 pounds of onions, 1,300 pickles, 3,500 loaves of bread, 32,000 cups of coffee, 25,000 grapefruit, and 6,000 pounds of lemons and 1,000 pounds of sugar for lemonade. Once lunch was over, the streets around the Mansion were roped off, and the crowd that grew to more than twenty-five thousand danced to the music of the hillbilly bands the governor loved.

Between the two inaugurations and following the second, the Mansion went through the most active and frenetic period in its history. The crowds continued to trample the lawns and gardens, particularly after O'Daniel began making statewide broadcasts from the parlor each Sunday morning. He concluded these programs with an open invitation to Texans to come and see him. School children got a special invitation to visit their governor, and they came by the bus load daily.

Merle O'Daniel held open house once a week and dinners and receptions of one kind or another at least that often. The O'Daniel offspring, all students at the University of Texas, had their friends from the campus to the Mansion for parties.

However, the biggest social event by far—and the largest ever held at the house—was the wedding of nineteen-year-old Molly O'Daniel. Once again, Governor O'Daniel invited all of Texas to see his daughter wed, and some twenty-five thousand came. Fewer than a hundred and fifty were able to get inside for the actual wedding, but the ceremony was carried to the grounds and surrounding streets by loudspeakers. The one-hundred-fifty-pound, three-tiered wedding cake was not enough to go around, but bakers had also prepared thousands of pounds of single layers.

The Mansion galas of the O'Daniel era ended in the summer of 1941 when the governor ran for the U.S. Senate seat left vacant by the death of Senator Morris Sheppard. His successor as thirty-fifth governor was Lieutenant Governor Coke Stevenson, a Hill Country rancher almost as taciturn as O'Daniel was gregarious. There were few festivities when he was sworn in on August 8, 1941, because his wife, Fay, was dying of cancer. She courageously attended the ceremony in the house of representatives in a wheelchair.

The Mansion became hospital quiet the day the Stevensons moved in. Fay Stevenson, weak from a months-long illness that she knew was terminal, was not able to host any kind of social affair. The Green Room downstairs had to be converted into a bedroom for her. A half bath was added and an elevator installed for her convenience when a rare trip to the living quarters upstairs was necessary. She died January 3, 1942.

Mrs. Stevenson is remembered as being gregarious and friendly. She had been a talented artist and an active sportswoman. She was an excellent public speaker and was an effective campaigner for her husband.

Following her death, the Stevenson's only son, Coke, Jr., and his wife, Scottie, moved into the Mansion with their two young daughters. During the remaining four-and-a-half years that Stevenson was governor, Scottie was the surrogate first lady. However, because of Fay's death and the restrictions on food and other supplies caused by World War II, there was limited entertaining.

When Stevenson left the office in 1947, he was succeeded by Beauford H. Jester as the thirty-sixth governor. He and his wife, Mabel, and their two youngest children moved into the Mansion

Governor Beauford Jester and his family pose in front of the Mansion following his January 21, 1947, inauguration. From left right are son-in-law Howard Burris, daughter Barbara, Governor Jester's mother, Governor Jester, First Lady Mabel Jester, daughter Joan, and son Beauford, Jr.

on January 21. By then the war was over, and the usual dinners, receptions, and parties were resumed.

Like other first ladies, Mabel Jester had her own ideas about how to make the Mansion more suited to the needs of her family. She converted the sleeping porches that had been on the west side into a suite of rooms—a bedroom, sitting room, bath, and a large cedar storage closet. She also added a small kitchen and dinette to the second floor family quarters.

Jester did not fill out his full term. En route to Houston by train, a Pullman porter found him in his berth dead from a heart attack on July 11, 1949. He is the only governor to die while serving in the office.

Jester's unexpected death moved Allan Shivers, then serving his second term as lieutenant governor, into the office of chief executive. He was to finish Jester's term and serve three of his own as the thirty-seventh governor.

In the more than seven years that Shivers, his wife, Marialice, and their three children (a fourth was born in 1952) lived in the Mansion, the house was to see many changes. As Marialice described it, "Things were in pitiful condition; draperies and

The Shivers family posed on the Mansion stairway in 1955 as Shivers began his third full term as governor. From left to right Marialice Sue (Cissie), AIlan, Jr. (Bud), First Lady Marialice Shivers, John, Brian, and Governor Allan Shivers. Brian was born on August 15, 1952, during the Shivers governorship.

During the Christmas season, First Lady Marialice Shivers posed in the newly decorated State Dining Room. Red flocked wallpaper had replaced the Zuber scenic paper, and an elegant crystal chandelier hung above the dining table acquired by Miss Ima Hogg.

curtains hanging in shreds; plumbing and heating pipes exposed."

Beginning with the foundation, which got new bracing, Mrs. Shivers had a new steel roof installed and recessed the wiring and pipes. A new central heating system replaced the old one, and for the first time, the Mansion was air conditioned.

The new roof was especially needed. In an interview nine years after the family left the Mansion, Mrs. Shivers recalled how badly the old roof had leaked. "I would have to go down to the kitchen for pans to catch the water—it wasn't just a drip, it poured."

The entire Mansion was redecorated, and many new furnishings were acquired. She ordered new silver flatware and china, establishing official state patterns for the first time in history. First Lady Marialice Shivers used many of her own lovely accessories in the house and encouraged others to donate gifts to the

Governor Price Daniel and his family moved into the Mansion in 1957. From left to right: Governor Daniel, daughter Jean, son John, First Lady Jean Houston Daniel, and sons Houston, and Price, Jr.

state. The Mansion received beautiful paintings, furnishings, and accessories.

Despite the hard work and expense lavished on the Mansion during the long administration of Shivers, there were still problems when his successor, Price Daniel, his wife, Jean, and their family moved in on January 15, 1957. The Daniels had been residents for only a few weeks when a large chunk of plaster fell from a hall ceiling, barely missing the thirty-eighth governor and some guests. Again the problem was the foundation, and this time, Jean Daniel studied the original architectural records before calling for repairs.

The Governor's Mansion was a major interest of Mrs. Daniel. One hundred years before she moved into the house as first lady, her ancestors lived there. Mrs. Daniel was the great-great- granddaughter of Margaret and Sam Houston. Being closely involved with the Mansion inspired Mrs. Daniel to gather all available information on the history of the house. She found much was missing on the background and history of the furnishings, some of them valuable antiques. After extensive research, *Furnishings of Historic Interest in the Governor's Mansion* was published in 1962. Both Governor and Mrs. Daniel continued their study of Mansion history, and with Dorothy Blodgett, compiled a

Governor John Connally posed with his wife Nellie, daughter Sharon, and younger son Mark for this 1963 Christmas photo. Governor Connally's arm is still in a sling, a month after the Kennedy assassination. John, the Connallys' oldest child, is not pictured.

complete history of the house and its occupants. *The Texas Governor's Mansion* was published in 1984.

Marialice Shivers had gathered together mementos left by some of the governors and placed them in a breakfront. The collection was further enlarged after a systematic search by Jean Daniel in 1957. Priceless heirlooms from earlier governors' families were added to what is now an outstanding feature of the Governor's Mansion.

Governor Daniel tried for an unprecedented fourth term in 1962 and lost. The victor, John B. Connally, became the thirty-ninth governor. He and his wife, Idanell, and their three children moved into the Mansion in 1963.

The Connallys found the Mansion still had problems. The fireplaces were beautiful, but not one of them functioned. If more than twelve people came to a state dinner, there was a problem in seating them. Things were even worse in the kitchen where the staff stumbled over each other trying to prepare a meal in the cramped quarters.

It was during the six-year stay of the Connallys that the Mansion once again had to serve as a hospital, as it had during the residency of the Coke Stevensons. This time, however, it was the governor rather than the first lady who was put to bed. He was

141

Mrs. John Connally displays the Mansion silver collection for an Austin American-Statesman *photographer in November 1968. Mrs. Connally, following the example of Mrs. Shivers and Mrs. Daniel, was active in soliciting donations of silver pieces for Mansion entertaining.*

gravely wounded while riding with President John F. Kennedy when the latter was assassinated in Dallas in November 1963.

"The building felt such a tremendous change of mood in such a short while," Mrs. Connally recalled. "For days we had excitedly planned for the visit of the President and Mrs. Kennedy to Austin. Then, in a moment it seems, the Mansion had become a somber and dreary place."

Governor Connally recovered, and the Mansion began to hum with visitors again. The children's laughter and First Lady Idanell (Nellie) Connally's personality added warmth and sparkle to the house.

Generous Texans donated many additional silver serving pieces to the Mansion Collection during the Connally administration. Mrs. Connally encouraged these gifts, and she increased the silver table service to sixty place settings.

However, Nellie Connally's most siguificant contribution to the Governor's Mansion was her dedication to making the setting of the Governor's Mansion one of the loveliest in the nation. The first lady's landscaping project, approved by the new Texas Fine Arts Commission and aided by the Texas Garden Clubs,

Inc., resulted in the beautiful Mansion grounds still evident today.

When Connally decided not to seek a fourth term, he was succeeded by Lieutenant Governor Preston Smith. The Smiths moved into the Mansion on January 21, 1969, for four years that added some unusual footnotes to the history of the house. There were the usual, expected social events that he and First Lady Ima Mae Smith were pleased to host. However, this was the era of unrest across the country, particularly on college campuses, and the Mansion did not escape.

There had been a tranquil period long ago when not a single guard was posted at the residence of the governor. However, as time passed and more and more visitors came, a Texas Ranger had been stationed there as a precaution. During the residence of the Connallys, the Department of Public Safety had increased its protection by adding patrolmen around the clock, and electronic devices had been added to protect the governor and his family. As far back as the tenancy of the James Allreds, there had been threats against the chief executive. However, it was not until the administration of Governor Smith that extra precautions had to be taken.

This was a time of sit-ins and marches and protests of all kinds. The number of threatening letters and telephone calls increased. Once a bomb was thrown into the Mansion gardens, the first such violence ever recorded during more than a century.

Governor and Mrs. Preston Smith posed in the Mansion Entry Hall with Mansion security officers and their wives (December 13, 1972).

Grafitti, most of it unprintable, appeared on the brick walls around the grounds.

For the first time, gates were installed at all entrances and locked. State troopers were deployed to the roof and galleries, rifles at the ready. The Smiths were carefully briefed on what to do in case of a terrorist attack. Fortunately, no real crisis ever developed, and the Smiths were unscathed when they moved out of the Mansion, and Dolph Briscoe became the forty-first governor on January 16, 1973.

Briscoe and his wife, Janey, were the first "team" to occupy the Mansion since Dan and Mildred Moody won the office in their "honeymoon campaign" of 1926. At almost every stop in Briscoe's tour of the state, his wife was with him. And when he moved into the governor's office at the Capitol, she had a desk there, too.

By the time the Briscoes moved into the Mansion, most of the tensions of the 1960s had eased, and their stay was a tranquil one. In addition to serving as a constant aide to the governor, his wife also undertook the task of redecorating his office. The private office of the governor ended up with a gorgeous Oriental rug on the floor, Victorian furniture "borrowed" from their ranch, and even a rocking chair to lull visitors.

The Briscoes made a major addition to the Mansion-a large wood-burning fireplace in the upstairs of the 1914 wing. Mrs.

On December 29, 1973, Janey Briscoe became the seventh governor's daughter to marry at the Governor's Mansion. Governor Dolph Briscoe escorted the oldest of his three children down the stairway to the ceremony.

First Lady Rita Clements posed in the Small Parlor for a Texas Homes *article on the completion of the Mansion restoration project.*

Briscoe acquired with state funds several fine antique chandeliers and light fixtures that were a significant addition to the Mansion Collection. During the Briscoe administration, the Texas Commission on the Arts and Humanities hired William Seale, a nationally known consultant on American decorative arts, to research the Governor's Mansion history and to propose an interior furnishing and decorative plan based on his research.

Briscoe was reelected in 1974 for a four-year term. The voters had approved an amendment to the constitution, effective in 1974, extending the term of office from two years to four. Both Dolph and Janey Briscoe liked their jobs and enjoyed public service. In 1978, he decided to try for another four-year term. In the Democratic primary, however, he lost to Attorney General John Hill. In turn, Hill was defeated in the general election by William P. Clements, Jr., the first Republican to be elected governor since Edmund J. Davis 110 years before.

It was Bill Clements, Texas' forty-second governor, and his wife, Rita, who were to spend more than half of his four-year term making the Executive Mansion the showplace every occupant of the house since Elisha M. Pease had wanted it to be. The Clements were willing to live for thirty months in a high-rise apartment and spent $4.1 million (more than three-fourths of it from private donations) to make the house the home they felt

Large Parlor

With the notable exception of the Belter sets in the parlors, the majority of the pieces seen in these 1979 photographs remain in the Mansion today.

In March of 1976, Janey and Dolph Briscoe accepted the plaque designating the Governor's Mansion a National Historic Landmark. Ernest A. Connally of the National Park Service, U.S. Department of the Interior, made the presentation.

Library

Conservatory

Small Parlor

Entry Hall

Texans wanted it to be. It is, after all, the fourth oldest Governor's Mansion among the fifty states.

First Lady Rita Clements was involved in every aspect of the renovation and restoration. The governor was also deeply interested in preserving the historical quality of the Mansion. They both inspired the people of the state to support this major project.

At Clements's request, the Sixty-sixth Legislature started the project in 1979 with a million-dollar appropriation to repair the structural defects on a house that originally cost only seventeen thousand dollars. There was much more, however, that the Clements felt was needed. They organized a nonprofit corporation called the FRIENDS OF THE GOVERNOR'S MANSION, through which Texans could contribute to the project.

The "new" Mansion officially opened April 2, 1982. Governor and Mrs. Clements, having lived in the Mansion only seven months before the renovation began, had moved back in January to oversee the finishing touches. Their stay, however, was to be short. In the 1982 elections, Clements lost his reelection bid, and Mark White became the forty-third governor of Texas.

Governor and Mrs. Bill Clements invited the former governors and their wives to dinner in the newly restored Governor's Mansion in the spring of 1982. Left to right: Governor and Mrs. Allan Shivers, Governor and Mrs. Price Daniel, Governor and Mrs. John Connally, Governor and Mrs. Preston Smith, Governor and Mrs. Dolph Briscoe, and Governor and Mrs. Bill Clements.

Governor and Mrs. Mark White pose with their family on the front lawn of the Governor's Mansion. Pictured from left to right are Wells White, First Lady Linda Gale White, Elizabeth White, Governor White, and Andrew White.

Governor Mark White and his wife, Linda Gale, brought young children back into the Governor's Mansion when their family moved in on January 18, 1983. Wells, Andrew, and Elizabeth were twelve, ten, and eight years old at the time. Even though the Mansion had been recently restored, the challenges of family life in such a public building continued.

*The Whites' sons used the Pease Bedroom as their personal bedroom, storing their toys and personal belongings out of sight of the frequent tour groups. Governor and Mrs. White hosted parties for their children and their friends. On several occasions, furniture was cleared from the State Dining Room to make room for dancing.

---

* The following text and photographs relating to the administrations from 1985 to 1997 were expanded by FRIENDS OF THE GOVERNOR'S MANSION for the 1997 edition.

Just months after the Whites moved into the newly renovated Mansion, a leak in a hot water line above the new public restrooms caused extensive steam and water damage to those rooms. Then a month later, in June of 1983, a portion of the ornate plaster cove in the large parlor crashed to the floor. It fell from the weight of debris that had accumulated during the many upstairs repair and renovation projects over the years. Craftsmen used undamaged sections as models to reproduce the plaster cove and repair the damaged area.

Governor and Mrs. White opened the Governor's Mansion to many visitors by increasing the number of tours given and by hosting receptions for numerous organized groups. Mrs. White began the Docents of the Governor's Mansion Program in 1983 under the auspices of the FRIENDS OF THE GOVERNOR'S MANSION. Over a hundred volunteers from Austin were trained during the first year of the program. These volunteers give tours and hostess public functions at the Mansion. To insure careful maintenance of the Mansion, Governor and Mrs. White retained the position of Mansion Administrator created by Governor and Mrs. Clements.

The 1986 election was a rematch of the candidates from four years earlier but the result was different: William P. Clements, Jr. defeated Mark White. In January, 1987, Rita and Bill Clements moved back into the Governor's Mansion they had helped restore. Mrs. Clements continued her active interest in the Mansion Collection. Two important 19th-century oil paintings by Texas artists, a portrait by Friedrich Richard Petri and a landscape by Hermann Lungkwitz, were acquired for the Mansion Collection during the Clements' second term.

This ornament from the County Christmas Ornament collection represents Bexar County and depicts historic sites in San Antonio.

Rita and Bill Clements welcomed many visitors to the Governor's Mansion for holiday events during their second term. The Christmas tree in the Large Parlor was always a highlight of the season.

The popular tours of the Mansion and gardens continued, with thousands of people visiting each year. The Christmas seasons, with holiday decorations outside and throughout the downstairs rooms, were a special time for visitors. Rita Clements created the collection of County Christmas Ornaments from each Texas county for the Mansion tree. These balls were handpainted between 1989 and 1991 by two hundred Texas artists with scenes of historic buildings and sites in their counties.

After a second four-year term in the Governor's Mansion, Bill Clements decided not to seek another term. Ann Richards was elected in 1990 and became the second woman to serve as Governor of Texas, following Miriam Ferguson by 56 years. Her inauguration featured a walking parade of thousands of Texans down Congress Avenue, led by Governor Richards herself. Her term became known as "The New Texas." Governor Richards appointed more minorities and women to state posts than any previous governor. Her administration saw new laws on ethics for officeholders and lobbyists, and an emphasis on public education financing.

Although there was no first lady to serve the traditional role as hostess, Governor Richards hosted many groups in the Mansion and often expressed her appreciation to Texans for letting her live in "the people's house." Her family, including four grown children and four grandchildren, joined her for family and special occasions in the Mansion, including the weddings of her two sons, Dan and Clark.

On May 20, 1991, Ann Richards welcomed Her Royal Majesty Queen Elizabeth II to a reception at the Governor's Mansion. Although Prince Charles came to the Mansion in 1986 for the Sesquicentennial celebration of Texas Independence, this was the first visit by a reigning British monarch to the Governor's

Queen Elizabeth II and Governor Ann Richards enter the Governor's Mansion for a reception in the Queen's honor. Behind them are Prince Philip and Texas Secretary of State John Hannah.

Governor George Bush and First Lady Laura Bush often enjoy activities on the Mansion grounds with their daughters Jenna and Barbara, and family dog Spot.

Mansion. Another international event took place when President-elect Bill Clinton met with President Carlos Salinas de Gortari of Mexico at the Mansion. Governor Richards invited the two leaders to meet upstairs in the private quarters, an informal setting for discussing economic and other issues important to Texas, Mexico and the United States.

Hours after being sworn in as the forty-sixth governor on January 17, 1995, George W. Bush and his wife, Laura Welch Bush, moved into the Governor's Mansion with their thirteen-year-old twin daughters, Barbara and Jenna. The Mansion was again alive with the sights and sounds of a young, active family.

Since the private quarters were not yet ready on moving day, the Bush family spent their first nights in the Pease and Sam Houston Bedrooms. Governor Bush later remarked that living amid the personal belongings and artifacts of Texas' great hero, Sam Houston, really underscored the historical significance of his new role as Governor. Ten days after taking office, Governor Bush signed his first bill into law in the Library of the Mansion.

First Lady Laura Bush's new life in the Mansion sparked in her a strong kinship with the former first ladies of Texas. A former public school librarian, Mrs. Bush has encouraged the expansion and preservation of the Mansion's collection of Texana for future generations to enjoy. Mrs. Bush has also promoted the work of Texas artists and authors. As a tribute to Texas folk artists, Mrs. Bush adorned the Mansion and its 15-foot Christmas tree in 1996 with hundreds of miniature wood carvings. The festive decorating was memorialized in a watercolor painting reproduced on the family's 1996 Christmas card.

The Bushs' visitors have included boxing heavyweight George Foreman, evangelist Billy Graham, El Paso artist Tom Lea, General Colin Powell and all the members of the extended Bush family, including the governor's parents, former President George Bush and First Lady Barbara Bush.

The Mansion also became home to the Bush's dog Spot, and two cats, Cowboy and India. After spending his first week at the Mansion hiding out in the Governor's closet, Cowboy got over his new-home jitters and joined India for daily prowls around the grounds. During one press conference in front of the Mansion, Cowboy sauntered up to the state and national journalists assembled to show off his catch of the day—a pigeon.

Visitors who tour the Mansion may catch glimpses of the family going about their everyday lives—the twins heading off to high school, the first lady in the formal garden talking with friends, or Governor Bush swatting tennis balls across the lawn for Spot, an English Springer Spaniel who was born in the White House to President and Mrs. Bush's dog, Millie.

Today, the house that Abner Cook designed as the residence for Texas heads of state in 1856 remains one of the most beautiful residences of its kind in the United States. It may not exactly fit the needs of each resident, but it is comfortable on the interior and beautiful on the exterior. Texans like it, and so have most of the First Families who have called it home.

Governors & First Ladies of Texas

Prior to Construction of the Governor's Mansion

James Pinckney Henderson	1846–1847
Frances Cox Henderson	
George T. Wood	1847–1849
Martha Evans Gindrat Wood	
Peter Hansborough Bell	1849–1853
James Wilson Henderson	1853

Occupants of the Governor's Mansion — **Terms of Office**

Elisha Marshall Pease — December 21, 1853–December 21, 1857
  Lucadia Christiana Niles Pease

Hardin R. Runnels — December 21, 1857–December 21, 1859

Sam Houston — December 21, 1859–March 16, 1861
  (resigned because of state's secession)
  Margaret Moffette Lea Houston

Edward Clark — March 16, 1861–November 7, 1861
  (Lt. Gov. succeeding Houston)
  Martha Melissa Evans Clark

Francis R. Lubbock — November 7, 1861–November 5, 1863
  (resigned to enter Confederate Army)
  Adele Baron Lubbock

*Pendleton Murrah — November 5, 1863–June 17, 1865
  (administration terminated by fall of
  Confederacy)
  Sue Ellen Taylor Murrah

Andrew J. Hamilton — July 21, 1865–August 9, 1866
  (provisional, appointed by President
  Johnson)
  Mary Jane Bowen Hamilton

James Webb Throckmorton — August 9, 1866–August 8, 1867
  Ann Rattan Throckmorton

Elisha Marshall Pease — August 8, 1867–September 30, 1869
  (appointed July 30, 1867 under martial
  law; did not move into the Mansion.
  Pease resigned and vacated office
  September 30, 1869. No successor was
  named until January 8, 1870)

Edmund Jackson Davis — January 8, 1870–January 15, 1874
  (appointed provisional governor after
  being elected)
  Anne Elizabeth Britton Davis

Richard Coke — January 15, 1874–December 1, 1876
  (resigned to enter United States Senate)
  Mary Evans Horne Coke

Richard B. Hubbard — December 1, 1876–January 21, 1879
  (Lt. Gov. succeeding Coke)
  Janie Roberts Hubbard

Oran M. Roberts — January 21, 1879–January 16, 1883
  Frances Wickliffe Edwards Roberts

John Ireland — January 16, 1883–January 18, 1887
  Anne Maria Penn Ireland

Lawrence Sullivan Ross — January 18, 1887–January 20, 1891
  Elizabeth Dorothy Tinsley Ross

*On Murrah's departure, Lt. Gov. Fletcher S. Stockdale (acting governor May–June 1865) performed some duties of the governor's office and is sometimes listed as governor, although Hamilton's appointment was for immediate succession.

James Stephen Hogg	January 20, 1891–January 15, 1895
Sarah Ann Stinson Hogg	
Charles A. Culberson	January 15, 1895–January 17, 1899
Sallie Harrison Culberson	
Joseph Draper Sayers	January 17, 1899–January 20, 1903
Orline Walton Sayers	
Samuel Willis Tucker Lanham	January 20, 1903–January 15, 1907
Sarah Beona Meng Lanham	
Thomas Mitchell Campbell	January 15, 1907–January 17, 1911
Fannie Irene Bruner Campbell	
Oscar Branch Colquitt	January 17, 1911–January 19, 1915
Alice Fuller Murrell Colquitt	
James E. Ferguson *(impeached)*	January 19, 1915–August 25, 1917
Miriam Amanda Wallace Ferguson	
William Pettus Hobby	August 25, 1917–January 18, 1921
(Lt. Gov. succeeding Ferguson)	
Willie Chapman Cooper Hobby	
Pat Morris Neff	January 18, 1921–January 20, 1925
Myrtle Mainer Neff	
Miriam A. Ferguson	January 20, 1925–January 17, 1927
Dan Moody	January 17, 1927–January 20, 1931
Mildred Paxton Moody	
Ross S. Sterling	January 20, 1931–January 17, 1933
Maud Abbie Gage Sterling	
Miriam A. Ferguson	January 17, 1933–January 15, 1935
James V. Allred	January 15, 1935–January 17, 1939
Joe Betsy Miller Allred	
W. Lee O'Daniel	January 17, 1939–August 4, 1941
(resigned to enter U.S. Senate)	
Merle Estelle Butcher O'Daniel	
Coke R. Stevenson	August 4, 1941–January 21, 1947
(Lt. Gov. succeeding O'Daniel)	
Blanch Fay Wright Stevenson	
Beauford Halbert Jester *(died in office)*	January 21, 1947–July 11, 1949
Mabel Buchanan Jester	
Allan Shivers	July 11, 1949–January 15, 1957
(Lt. Gov. succeeding Jester)	
Marialice Shary Shivers	
Price Daniel	January 15, 1957–January 15, 1963
Jean Houston Baldwin Daniel	
John B. Connally	January 15, 1963–January 21, 1969
Idanell Brill Connally	
Preston Smith	January 21, 1969–January 16, 1973
Ima Mae Smith Smith	
Dolph Briscoe, Jr.	January 16, 1973–January 16, 1979
Betty Jane Slaughter Briscoe	
William P. Clements, Jr.	January 16, 1979–January 18, 1983
Rita Crocker Clements	
Mark Wells White	January 18, 1983–January 20, 1987
Linda Gale Thompson White	
William P. Clements, Jr.	January 20, 1987–January 15, 1991
Rita Crocker Clements	
Ann Willis Richards	January 15, 1991–January 17, 1995
George Walker Bush	January 17, 1995–
Laura Welch Bush	

Illustration Credits

Front Cover: Bill Records, Austin

Back Cover: Hickey Robertson Photographers, Houston

p. ii: Hickey Robertson Photographers, Houston

p. vi: Texas Department of Transportation

p. 1: Hendricks and Walls Inc., Dallas

p. 2–6: Hickey Robertson Photographers, Houston

p. 7 (top right): Eric Beggs, Austin

p. 7–19: Hickey Robertson Photographers, Houston

p. 19 (bottom): Eric Beggs, Austin

p. 20–44: Hickey Robertson Photographers, Houston

p. 45–54: Robert Anschutz and Terry Duff, Austin; Nos. 50 and 52, Larry Schiller, Austin; Nos. 47 and 48, Eric Beggs, Austin

p. 55: AHC* AF-Governor's Mansion General G3800 (1) PICA 06526

p. 56: Texas State Library 1982/313–9

p. 57–61: Hendricks and Walls, Inc., Dallas

p. 62–63: Hendricks and Walls, Inc., Dallas

p. 65: Mansion Collection, Austin

p. 66: Texas Department of Transportation

p. 66: Texas State Library 1/103–506

p. 69: Courtesy Texas General Land Office, Austin

p. 71: AHC AF-Austin-Pictures, Illustrations (1840–1879) A8700 PICA 01083

p. 72: AHC AF-Streets-Congress Ave.-1870 S5710 C00393

p. 73: Texas State Library 1932/5–21

p. 75: AHC AF-BIO Cook, Abner PICB 01890

p. 75: Hendricks and Walls, Inc., Dallas

p. 76: Courtesy Ladies' Hermitage Association, Hermitage, Tennessee

p. 78: AHC AF-Niles Road 6 PICH 02200

p. 78: AHC HB-6TH W. 1008 PICH 00296 *detail shown*

p. 79: Texas State Library, Adair Collection, 1963/283–63

p. 79: AHC HB-San Gabriel 2310 PICH 002766

p. 80: *American Builder's Companion,* Title Page

p. 80: *American Builder's Companion,* Plates F & G

p. 82: Texas State Library 1932/5–50

p. 84: Texas State Library 1932/5–105

p. 87: AHC AF-Governor's Mansion General G3800 (1) PICA 06530

p. 88: AHC AF-Governor's Mansion General G3800 (1) PICA 08734

p. 89: AHC AF-Governor's Mansion General G3800 (1) PICA 06523

p. 90: AHC AF-BIO Neff, Pat Morris C08031

p. 90: AHC AF-BIO Moody, Daniel J. C02871

p. 91: AHC AF-CHILDREN General C2800 PICA 08556

p. 92: AHC AF-BIO Moody, Daniel J. C02865

p. 92: Texas State Library 1976/8–92

p. 93: Bill Malone, Austin; AHC MB 65522

p. 95: Texas State Library 1964/306–168 & 1964/275–3

p. 95: AHC AF-BIO Pease, Lucadia C. PICB 06779

p. 99: Mansion Collection, Austin

p. 101: Texas Department of Transportation

p. 103: AHC AF-Governor's Mansion General G3800 (1) PICA 08592 *detail shown*

p. 107: AHC HB-Niles Road 6 PICH 02194 *detail shown*

p. 108: AHC AF-MAPS M100 (4) Austin C00120 *detail shown*

p. 112: AHC AF-Austin Pictures, Illustrations (1880–1889) A8701 PICA 01095

p. 113: Center for American History, University of Texas at Austin

p. 116: Photoengraving from Pearl Jackson's book, *Texas Governor's Wives*

p. 116: Center for American History, University of Texas at Austin, CN00307 & CN00953

p. 119: AHC AF-Governor's Mansion General G3800 (1) C2730

p. 120: Center for American History, University of Texas at Austin, CN00339

p. 120: Same, CN00952

p. 122: AHC AF-BIO Ferguson, James E. C02883

p. 122: AHC AF-BIO Ferguson, James E. C02569

p. 126: Courtesy of Mrs. Edward E. Stocker, Fort Worth

p. 127: Same

* Austin History Center

p. *127–128:* Courtesy of Mrs. Edward E. Stocker, Fort Worth

p. *129:* AHC AF-BIO Neff, Pat Morris C03066

p. *129:* AHC AF-BIO Folder 1 Ferguson, James E.

p. *130:* AHC AF-Governor's Mansion General G3800 (1) PICA 06556 *detail shown*

p. *130:* AHC AF-BIO Moody, Daniel J. C02801 *detail shown*

p. *131:* Courtesy of Mrs. Walter G. Sterling, Houston

p. *132:* AHC AF-BIO Allred, James V. PICB 00001 *detail shown*

p. *132:* AHC AF-Governor's Mansion Interiors G3800 (2) PICA 06589 *detail shown*

p. *132:* AHC AF-BIO Allred, James V. PICB 00101

p. *133:* AHC AF-Governor's Mansion Interiors G3800 (2) PICA 06593 *detail shown*

p. *133:* HABS photos, Library of Congress, Emil Niggli, photographer; AHC AF-Governor's Mansion General G3800 (1) PICA 06552 *detail shown*

p. *133:* HABS photos, Library of Congress, Emil Niggli, photographer; AHC AF-Governor's Mansion General G3800 (1) PICA 06551 *detail shown*

p. *133:* AHC AF-Governor's Mansion Interiors G3800 (2) PICA 06590 *detail shown*

p. *135:* Texas State Library 1976/8–56

p. *135:* AHC AF-Governor's Mansion Interiors G3800 (2) PICA 06596

p. *136:* Texas State Library 1976/8–25

p. *136:* Texas State Library 1976/198–15

p. *138:* Texas State Library 1976/8–745

p. *139:* Texas State Library 1976/198–184

p. *139:* Bill Malone, Austin; AHC MB 60135

p. *140:* Texas State Library 1976/198–192

p. *141:* AHC Austin American-Statesman files

p. *142:* AHC Austin American-Statesman files

p. *143:* Texas State Library 1973/71–1

p. *144:* Texas State Library 1976/135–3

p. *145:* Hickey Robertson Photographers, Houston

p. *146:* Texas State Library 1974/83–56

p. *146:* Texas State Library 1980/13–11 & 1976/135–3

p. *147:* Texas State Library 1980/13–21, 1980/13–1, 1980/13–18 & 1980/13–14

p. *148:* Bill Malone, Austin

p. *149:* John Jefferson, Austin

p. *150:* Courtesy of Gov. & Mrs. William P. Clements, Jr.

p. *151:* Charles Guerrero, Austin

p. *152:* Nancy Whitworth, Austin

Bibliography

BOOKS AND OTHER SOURCES

Alexander, Drury Blakeley. *Texas Homes of the Nineteenth Century.* Austin: University of Texas Press, 1966.

Barker, Eugene C. *The Life of Stephen F. Austin.* Nashville-Dallas: Cokesbury Press, 1925.

Barker, Eugene C., ed. *The Austin Papers.* vols. 1 and 2. Washington, D.C.: Government Printing Office, 1924–1928. vol. 3. Austin: University of Texas Press, 1927.

Belo, A. H. *Texas Almanac 1947.* Dallas: A.H. Belo Corp., 1947.

Benner, Judith Ann. *Sull Ross—Soldier, Statesman, Educator.* College Station: Texas A&M University Press, 1983.

Benjamin, Asher. *The American Builder's Companion.* New York: Dover Publications, 1969.

Bjerkoe, Ethel Hall. *The Cabinetmakers of America.* Exton, Pa.: Schiffer, Ltd., 1957.

Bolton, Paul. *Governors of Texas.* San Angelo: *San Angelo Standard Times*, 1947.

Christian, Asa Kyrus. *Mirabeau Buonaparte Lamar.* Austin: Von BoeckmannJones, 1922.

Cotner, Robert C. *James Stephen Hogg, A Biography.* Austin: University of Texas Press, 1959.

Daniel, Jean Houston. *Furnishings of Historical interest in the Governor's Mansion.* Austin, 1962.

___. *The Governor's Collection.* Austin, 1962.

___. and Price Daniel. *Executive Mansions and Capitols of America.* Waukesha, Wis.: Country Beautiful, 1969.

___. Price Daniel, and Dorothy Blodgett. *The Texas Governor's Mansion.* Austin: Texas State Library and Archives Commission and the Sam Houston Regional Library and Research Center, 1984.

DeShields, James T. *They Sat in High Places: The Presidents and Governors of Texas.* San Antonio: The Naylor Co., 1940.

Farrell, Mary D., and Elizabeth Silverthorne. *First Ladies of Texas.* Belton: Stillhouse Hollow Publishers, 1976.

Friend, Llerena B. *Sam Houston: The Great Designer.* Austin: University of Texas Press, 1954.

Gambrell, Herbert. *Mirabeau Buonaparte Lamar, Troubador and Crusader.* Dallas: Southwest Press, 1934.

Gantt, Fred, Jr. *The Chief Executive in Texas.* Austin: University of Texas Press, 1964.

Hafertepe, Kenneth. *Abner Cook: Master Builder on the Texas Frontier.* Austin: Texas State Historical Association, 1992.

Hamer, Marcelle Lively. *The Governor's Mansion of Texas and Its Furnishings.* Austin, 1937.

Hart, Katherine, and Elizabeth Kemp. *Lucadia Pease and the Governor: Letters, 1850–1857.* Austin: Encino Press for the Friends of the Austin Public Library, 1974.

Hendrickson, Kenneth E., Jr. *The Chief Executives of Texas from Stephen F. Austin, to John B. Connally, Jr.* College Station: Texas A&M University Press, 1995.

Jackson, Pearl Cashell. *Texas Governor's Wives.* Austin: E.L. Steck Co., 1915.

James, Marquis. *The Raven: A Biography of Sam Houston.* Indianapolis: BobbsMerrill, 1929.

Johnson, Frank W. *A History of Texas and the Texans.* Chicago and New York: The American Historical Society, 1914.

LaFever, Minard. *The Modern Builder's Guide.* New Haven: Research Publications, Inc., 1972.

Maguire, Jack. "Governor's Day." *Southwest Airlines Magazine,* January 1977.

___. "When Texas Impeached a Governor. *Southwest Airlines Magazine,* September 1977.

___. "The Governors." *Southwest Airlines Magazine,* January 1979.

___. "The Mansion That's Not a Home." *Southwest Airlines Magazine,* June 1979.

___. "Two Governors for the Price of One." *Southwest Airlines Magazine,* February 1980.

___. "The Governor Who Wasn't." *Southwest Airlines Magazine,* November 1984.

___. *Texas: Amazing, But True.* Austin: Eakin Publications, 1985.

Moore, Walter B. *Governors of Texas.* Dallas: Dallas Morning News, 1969.

Newcomer, Velda. *Texas' First Ladies.* Denton: Texas Women's University, 1978.

Nichols, Frederick D. *The Architecture of Georgia.* Savannah: Beehive Press, 1976.

Nunn, W. C., ed. *Ten More Texans in Gray.* Hillsboro: Hill Junior College Press, 1980.

Paulissen, May Nelson, and Carl McQueary. *Miriam: The Southern Belle Who Became The First Woman Governor Of Texas.* Austin: Eakin Press, 1995.

Patrick, James. *Architecture in Tennessee, 1768–1897.* Knoxville: University of Tennessee Press, 1981.

Pease Letters. R. Niles Graham—Pease Collection. Austin History Center, Austin.

Phares, Ross. *The Governors of Texas.* Gretna, La.: Pelican Publishing Co., 1976.

Raines, C. W., ed. *Speeches and State Papers of James Stephen Hogg.* Austin: State Printing Co., 1905.

Ratcliffe, Sam DeShong. *Painting Texas History to 1900.* Austin: University of Texas Press, 1992.

Roberts, Madge Thornall. *Star of Destiny: The Private Life of Sam and Margaret Houston.* Denton: University of North Texas Press, 1993.

Ruffin, Lisa. "Open House: The Governor's Mansion Restored." *Texas Homes.* August 1982.

San Antonio Express, August 31, 1936.

Seale, William. "Report on the Texas Governor's Mansion, 1975." Texas Legislative Reference Library, Texas Capitol, Austin.

Smith, Joseph Frazer. *White Pillars.* New York: Branhall House, 1941.

Steely, Jim. "The Governor's Mansion." *Texas Highways,* February 1984.

Taylor, Lonn, and David B. Warren. *Texas Furniture.* Austin: University of Texas Press, 1975.

Turner, Martha Anne. *Richard Bennett Hubbard: An American Life.* Austin: Shoal Creek Publishers, 1979.

Tyler Ron, ed. *The Handbook of Texas.* 6 vols. Austin: Texas State Historical Association, 1996.

Wallace, Ernest, David M. Vigness, and George B. Ward, ed. *Documents of Texas History.* Austin: State House Press, 1994.

Wark, David Elmore. "Abner Hugh Cook-Master Builder and Citizen of Austin." Master's Thesis, University of Texas at Austin, 1981.

Welch, June Rayfield. *The Texas Governors.* Dallas: G.L.A. Press, 1977.

Williams, Amelia W., and Eugene C. Barker, eds. *The Writings of Sam Houston, 1813–1863.* 8 vols. Austin: Pemberton Press, 1970.

Collections

Austin History Center. Austin Public Library. Austin, Texas.

Center for American History. University of Texas at Austin. Austin, Texas.

FGM Curating Files. Friends of the Governor's Mansion. Austin, Texas.

Governor's Mansion Curating Files. Governor's Mansion. Austin, Texas.

Archives and Information Division—Texas State Library. Austin, Texas.

About the Authors

DRURY BLAKELEY ALEXANDER joined the faculty of the University of Texas at Austin in 1955. He was the Meadows Foundation professor of architecture and is now Professor Emeritus. Dr. Alexander was the recipient of the Eugene McDermott Lectureship in Architecture Award, 1983–1985, and is a past chairman of the City of Austin Historic Landmark Commission. His publications included *The Sources of Classicism: Five Centuries of Architectural Books* and *Texas Homes of the Nineteenth Century.*

JOE B. FRANTZ was a native Texan. He was a professor of history at the University of Texas, joining the faculty in 1949. He held numerous honorary positions, including director of the Texas State Historical Association and vice-chairman of the National Parks Service Advisory Board. He was the author of several acclaimed books on Texas history.

DEALEY DECHERD HERNDON was the Administrator of FRIENDS OF THE GOVERNOR'S MANSION from 1983 to 1984. She wrote and edited the first edition of this guidebook. Ms Herndon has subsequently served on the FRIENDS Board of Directors since 1985. As Executive Director of the State Preservation Board from 1991 to 1995, she was responsible for the award-winning restoration and extension of the Texas Capitol. Governor George W. Bush and the Texas Historical Commission honored her in 1997 with the Governor's Award for Historic Preservation. Ms. Herndon is a board member of the National Trust for Historic Preservation.

JACK MAGUIRE served as executive director of the University of Texas Institute of Texan Cultures from 1976 to 1985. A native of Denison, he has been writing about Texas for over sixty years. His weekly syndicated newspaper column, "Talk of Texas," began in 1962. He was a member of the Texas Sesquicentennial Commission. His publications include *A President's Country* (1965), *Talk of Texas* (1973), and *Texas, Amazing But True* (1985).

AUDRAY BATEMAN RANDLE became curator of the Austin History Center in 1975 and is now Curator Emeritus. Mrs. Randle received the Outstanding Service Award of the Society of Southwest Archivists in 1984 and was an ex-officio member of the Landmark Committee of the City of Austin. Mrs. Randle has served as an editor of Waterloo Press and wrote a newspaper column, "Waterloo Scrapbook," which appeared for many years in the *Austin American-Statesman.*

Cover design by BRADFIELD MARTINO INC.

Index